SAD
HAPPENS

A Celebration of Tears

Edited by

Brandon Stosuy

Illustrated by

Rose Lazar

Simon & Schuster

New York   London   Toronto   Sydney   New Delhi

Simon & Schuster
1230 Avenue of the Americas
New York, NY 10020

First Simon & Schuster hardcover edition November 2023

SIMON & SCHUSTER and colophon are registered trademarks of Simon & Schuster, Inc.

For information about special discounts for bulk purchases, please contact Simon & Schuster Special Sales at 1-866-506-1949 or business@simonandschuster.com.

The Simon & Schuster Speakers Bureau can bring authors to your live event. For more information or to book an event, contact the Simon & Schuster Speakers Bureau at 1-866-248-3049 or visit our website at www.simonspeakers.com.

Interior design by Ruth Lee-Mui

Manufactured in China

1   3   5   7   9   10   8   6   4   2

Library of Congress Cataloging-in-Publication Data has been applied for.

ISBN 978-1-6680-0345-9
ISBN 978-1-6680-0347-3 (ebook)

This book is dedicated to my mother,

Nancy Milne Haff (1947–2010),

who from the beginning to the

end, taught me it was okay to cry.

BRANDON STOSUY

This book is dedicated to all the

criers: thank you for your service.

ROSE LAZAR

Sad
Happens

Introduction

The Origins and Ongoing Story of Sad Happens

A number of years ago, I realized how many people were crying around me. It felt like it kept escalating. I wasn't sure if that was actually the case, though, or if it was the usual amount of crying people, and I'd just started to pay attention.

Once you start noticing something, you see more of it. Like when you go to a car wash, on the way home you might notice how everyone else's car looks dirty, even though you were driving a dirty car too just a few minutes ago and hadn't thought much of it.

What stuck with me was the variety of the situations. I saw folks crying in surprising settings (a guy crying in an art supply store), people crying in what turned out to be common settings (many, many people cry while jogging), people crying while doing something mundane (one guy while eating a corn muffin, a few others while vaping), and people who stuck out for other reasons (see: a guy wearing a homemade T-shirt emblazoned with the phrase YOU'VE GOT A FRIEND AT VERIZON).

I kept thinking about the gap between what I was witnessing in public and the private interiority that their tears acknowledged. I wanted to know their stories. *Why* were these people crying? Were they in the middle of an intractable conflict? Did they just get terrible news? Had they made it to the other side of a seemingly impossible situation? And, most importantly, what was up with the guy with the mohawk who cried as he ate chopped melon from a bodega fruit salad?

I started tweeting my random encounters with tears on the streets of New York, and to my surprise, tens of thousands of people started liking, retweeting, and commenting on my tweets, or DMing me about their own crying encounters. One particular tweet I'd sent out into the world, about someone crying on the subway, pausing to smile and take a selfie, and then crying again—a true story—currently has more than a million views.

Everybody cries, obviously, and so these things resonate. When you're the one crying you can feel quite alone, but you truly aren't. As I reported on what I saw, it turned into an unexpected way to find common ground with strangers. People related. On one hand, people feel a deep resonance with strangers when they see someone crying. Reading my tweets, they probably felt empathetic toward the picture the words conjured in their mind. Judging from all the crying and laughing emojis, they also maybe remembered times when they had cried in a less-than-ideal place: tears can be profound, but when their profundity meets a casual moment, it can quickly turn to absurdity.

Over a few years, I've posted about people crying hundreds of times. Some used a basic format of "guy crying" followed by how, when, or where I saw them crying. In other cases, I'd write about sad situations more generally. For some, I'd add the hashtag #holocene, a reference to a sad song, "Holocene," by the musician Bon Iver. It's one of those songs with largely indecipherable lyrics setting a mood for an expansively expressive backdrop that can make anything depressingly beautiful at a moment's notice—like the time I saw my old office's IT guy packing his bag just to leave for the day; "Holocene" started playing on my iTunes and I almost broke down.

I've spent a large part of my life listening to and writing about music. I started the "Holocene" hashtag one morning when I still worked at the online music publication *Pitchfork* and was surrounded by music as part of my nine-to-five job. (I made a joke about someone desperately doing push-ups the night before their high school reunion while listening to "Holocene," and it became internet shorthand for acknowledging a poignant moment). Music, especially the sort I'm drawn to, has a tendency to make anything feel like the climactic scene in a movie. It's why *I* cry so often when jogging and listening to Explosions in the Sky and why most movies have a song playing during their climactic scene. (It's worth noting that on my last day at *Pitchfork*, someone played "Holocene" over the office stereo as I walked out the door for the last time. It felt like the finale to some John Hughes film from the eighties.)

Back to my dispatches on tears: I had a few rules for posting. I never actually approached anyone who was crying; I didn't want to meddle. I also didn't ever want to make fun of anyone. The tweets were never mocking; they just explained what I saw, with no embellishments.

It's worth noting that I've only ever reported on "guys" crying, though I never specified if that person was male or female. I didn't do this to intentionally flip a stereotype; it just so happened that the first few people I saw crying were men, and so I stuck with it. That said, it did dawn on me pretty quickly that this choice to keep things gender-neutral made every story feel more relatable. For example, I'll tweet about "some guy" crying and both men and women will reply "that was me." And it is. That's part of what I like about this kind of writing: It's easy to see yourself in these various people— even if you've never cried while eating a corn muffin. I realized that when placed together, these tweets gained power. They were specific, yet universal; it felt like an ongoing narrative. Is it always the same "guy"? Is it all of us?

At some point a small press approached me about doing a poetry collection or chapbook based on the tweets. I reached out to my friend Rose to see if she'd help me illustrate it. I was curious what she'd see in the words I'd decided to jot down. I'd been inspired by people I saw, and I thought the book needed images as well. Visual art, like music, has a way of adding weight to just about any moment. I knew she'd be able to bring certain details into fuller focus for the reader.

We met up, and as we talked, we realized this should be a bigger project. We saw it as an opportunity to hear from artists and non-artists, friends and strangers, about their experiences of crying. In this way, we were able to paint a larger emotional landscape. Instead of snapshots without context, *Sad Happens* is the collective, multifaceted archive of tears it always needed to be. It became a way to get to the *why* of crying that had always interested me and that I'd never had the guts to ask about. In a way, Twitter provided the community, while the book format offered the possibility of going deeper.

Rose, who I've known for a long time, since we both lived in Buffalo, ended up illustrating each of the one hundred and fifteen stories in *Sad Happens* (including her own). She's a great friend: She came over and decorated my kid's room before he was born because I was in New Jersey with my wife at my mother's funeral. I arrived home from that sad trip to find a beautifully painted room, filled with framed illustrations of birds, mushrooms, and other magical little things. Both of my children grew up with her art on their walls. It's the first art they knew.

I've watched her businesses—Cosmic Peace Studio and the limited-edition press Aventures LTD, which she started with her husband, the musician Robert A.A. Lowe—grow in the most mellow, organic way. As much as her businesses have grown, her DIY ethos has remained. In her work, she references the past via song lyrics, movie quotes, and iconic symbols. There's a nostalgia to everything she creates, and I find that often when I cry, it's about something nostalgic—a friend I don't know so well anymore, how fast my kids are growing, the smell of cut grass that brings me back to my childhood. When Rose and I met to discuss this book in her studio, I mentioned some Adam Sandler comedy special I'd watched where he sang a song about Chris Farley, and we both got teary. This book is a logical extension of our shared sensibility (and sentimentality).

So, from the start, I thought of the book in terms of collaboration.

From there, the first person I asked to contribute was my old friend Matt Berninger. He's the singer of a band called the National, and we've known each other for more than twenty years. Before the National was big, long before they won a Grammy or he'd done a duet with Taylor Swift, I remember sitting in a bar in Manhattan and being handed a copy of the *Village Voice*; Matt was bummed that the National was getting tiny write-ups, while Interpol had a full page. His voice cracking, he worried they'd never be the band with a full-page feature in the *Village Voice*.

Matt's very well-known now for his very sad lyrics (for example, from the song "Sorrow": "Sorrow found me when I was young / Sorrow waited, sorrow won"), and his band has an album called *Sad Songs for Dirty Lovers*. So, yeah, Matt related to this project, sent me an essay, and then started reaching out to some of his friends whom he thought might want to contribute.

The second person I got in touch with, through Matt, was the musician Phoebe Bridgers. Her album *Stranger in the Alps* was the soundtrack of this book's early origins; it quite often made (and still makes) me cry. When I listened to it, it put me in the right mood to dig deep into my and other people's tears. It was fitting, too, considering the early tweet origins of the collection, that she writes about crying in public in her contribution to *Sad Happens*.

Then the floodgates opened.

Rose and I began asking a number of folks to participate. We hit up friends and friends of friends. Then I went back to where it all began and tweeted a request for submissions. The tweet read: "I'm working on a book about crying. I would love to hear from people who have jobs that maybe bring them in direct contact with tears: funeral directors, emergency response workers, fire fighters, florists, stay-at-home parents, etc. Please reach out via DM."

More than a hundred people responded, and their candor has made *Sad Happens* stronger, more comprehensive, *and* quirkier. This is also why the list of contributors now includes a bereavement counselor, an ICU nurse, a spin class instructor, a pet communicator, a bookstore employee, an investigative reporter, a vintage clothes seller, a florist, and a zookeeper.

All to say: This book is a collaboration, and it would not have worked if it was written by one person. It's a gathering of longtime friends and associates who have cried together, or maybe cried apart from each other. (We've laughed together too. Sometimes crying and laughing happen at the same time, or near each other, and I think you'll see that with this book too.) It's also a collaboration between me and relative strangers—people who saw my call for stories about crying and decided to let me—and you—into their lives.

·   ·   ·

Sad Happens has gotten bigger in scope because of its contributors, but even more because the project is meeting a moment. It's been a tough few years. And while every year could be tough—you never know the year that you'll lose your job or experience a profound loss—as we put this book together, it felt like things just kept imploding. We're living in a time of despair for many people—the pandemic, which brought an extraordinary loss of life; problematic Supreme Court rulings; war; the threat of climate castastrophe—and next to this we're all battling the usual stress of work, everyday life, relationships, parenthood. For many people, it's been harder to maintain balance or to want to keep going.

With that in mind, we plan to make a donation to benefit the Trevor Project, which provides suicide prevention and mental health crisis services to LGBTQ+ young people by phone, text, and chat. Through a toll-free telephone number, it operates the Trevor Lifeline, a confidential service that offers callers access to trained counselors. We'd like for *Sad Happens* to be a reading experience based on empathy and connectedness, and we'd also like to be able to help supply actual resources through sales of this book and this donation.

I tend to gravitate toward sad things. I wear black every day. My tattoos are all black. I think the Cure's *Disintegration* is the best album ever made. Whenever I go out for work or to meet friends, my two young sons sing "Cat's in the Cradle" to me. I'm a Buffalo Bills fan. I'm not really goth, though: I'm just someone who has a uniform, likes sad music, is raising my kids to have a dark sense of humor, and is a long-suffering sports fan.

But this isn't a sad book, despite what the title says. It should be cathartic. I hope it helps people. The shared emotion of *Sad Happens* has real power: It gives us permission to open up, let down our guard, embrace those things that make us feel vulnerable. By sharing, we see that crying is universal, and that tears should, in fact, be celebrated.

One thing to note: I wanted to remove any sort of hierarchy from *Sad Happens*—tears exist outside of rank and value—so the stories are listed in alphabetical order by the crier's last name. That's the order. In this way, *Sad Happens* feels like a dictionary or almanac of tears.

Recently, a friend of mine told me that she felt like I'd been writing this book since she met me twenty years ago, and the truth is, I've likely been writing it one way or another even longer.

I cried about a thousand times while putting it together.

Hanif Abdurraqib

(writer, poet)

The psychologist says that it is a perceived lack of control that triggers a sense of panic and helplessness in the brain. Another one says that it is the simple result of science: cabin pressure plus dehydration equals tears. All of this is supposed to explain why I have been on airplanes, staring into the creased leather on the back of a stranger's headrest, and fighting back tears while listening to a specific howl in a portion of a song I've heard endless times, never moving me toward any such fluorescent emotion when earthbound.

There is no shortage of crying on airplanes. Babies screech and moan through their assorted discomforts. People watch movies on small screens and put their hands over their mouths while a single tear descends. I've seen it, sure. I've tried to look away, but I've been there too. You and I have perhaps met there, in that rarified garden of weeping. I am not ashamed of crying in public. Yet there is something about having it happen on an airplane that feels jarring. For me, it arrives unexpectedly. I'm in a metal container, affixed to a seat among people who might recognize the rush of emotion but might not be all that interested in talking about it.

I don't want to combat science or psychology, but I would like to offer an alternative: If there is a heaven, and if it exists in the sky, and if it holds everyone I have loved and everyone I miss, it is certainly higher than the heights any airplane can reach. And yet, you are still suspended, well above any of the living people you love and also miss. Too high to touch the living, not high enough to be an audience to your beloved dead. I propose that this is the loneliest place. The body might not know it, but it doesn't matter. The heart rings the loudest bell. Everything else falls in line.

Farah Ali

(writer, author of People Want to Live*)*

Two years ago, my cat hurt his leg in a fight with another cat in the street. He is a Persian, rescued by a friend. She had found him on the terrace of a mosque, abandoned by his previous owner. His long hair was matted and dirty. He was just a little over a year old then. A week after my friend found him, I adopted him. When allowed to grow unchecked, Gizmo's hair can get wild and scraggly, getting up to three and a half inches long, the length of a crayon, blooming around his otherwise narrow body. Three vertical grooves on his forehead make him look slightly angry. But it's all deceptive, the size and the grooves. He does not like being in the dark by himself. He sleeps as close as possible to another human. A stray kitten once made him run the other way.

The fight wounded his leg. The gash was large and open. Palish red blood matted the hair around it. He walked with a limp. I took him to the vet, where he sat on my lap quietly while we waited. Unlike other times at the vet, he wasn't fidgety; the pain from his wound made him lose interest in the objects around him. At home, I realized I had forgotten to buy his medicine. I sat again in the car. I only drove for a minute before beginning to cry. There was no preamble of gentle weeping or sniffling. Straightaway, it was a loud, ugly wail. I was crying so hard I could not see and had to pull over. The force of the sobbing made my ribs ache. Then, the part of me that was observing this drama from above said to me with cool detachment, *This is really about your father, you know.*

My father had passed away a few months before this. In the forty-five minutes between getting a phone call that he wasn't doing well and rushing home to pack a bag to get on a plane, he had died.

For weeks afterward I would get in the car and, if alone, begin to bawl. I had cried on the way to a reading, on the way back from a run, on the way to the supermarket.

Crying me argued, *This time, it's the cat,* but the floating me said, *No, it's your father.* I was angry now. Astral-projection me was observing me, making me feel like a spectacle. I stayed in the car until I could see again. Ultimately, the other me disappeared. I bought the ointment the cat needed. I went home. Banalities took over.

I haven't cried like that for my father for a while. I would like to know that it's because it's been two years since he died and because grief has a natural path. But grief does not recognize time or logical causation. Being alive means losing people and, like in the Peter Gabriel song "I Grieve," "life carries on in the people I meet."

Nada Alic

(writer, author of Bad Thoughts*)*

In the weeks leading up to the release of my first book, I was working morning to night on endless administrative tasks while seated in the least ergonomic position: usually in bed or on the couch, with my neck strained forward and my wrists bent. I was in constant pain and being a big baby about it, so my friend suggested I visit a day spa in a little plaza near my house for a deep tissue massage. I'd never had a deep tissue massage (due to being a big baby), but my pain felt intense enough to warrant this kind of medical intervention. I approached the experience like an athlete recovering from training, except that my injuries were caused by staring at my computer for too long. (I hoped no one would be able to tell the difference, and maybe be impressed.)

A few minutes into the massage, something strange started happening to me: tears began leaking out of my face. These were not tears from physical pain, but from some deep primal wound that had been dislodged from my shoulder. The elderly woman kneaded my spine with her bare elbow, the tears turned to sobs. I suddenly had no control over what my face was doing; it felt less like I was crying than that crying was happening to me.

As a writer, I've chosen a life of the mind to the exclusion of the body, so whatever it's up to feels like none of my business. In the spirit of efficiency, I do my best not to waste whatever metabolic process is required to generate tears, and, instead, I prefer to overthink something into submission or repress, repress, repress. If I must cry, it's usually in private where I will let it out quickly, like a sneeze. My massage cry betrayed all of my bodily protocols.

Halfway through my massage/emotional exorcism, my initial embarrassment gave way to relief. I'd been holding in so much over the last few months: the grief of letting my book go, the fear of what will happen to it, and the loneliness of writing it over the last three years. Instead of feeling it, I tried to work my way through it. But as they say, the body (annoyingly) does keep the score. I surrendered to it and wept uncontrollably; the massage therapist said nothing, but she laughed in a maternal way. I then understood that she made people cry all the time. She saw my pain and didn't judge me. When it was over, I cried in the parking lot, and on the drive home. I kept driving and crying and I didn't even cover my face. I came home and cried in the shower; I just kept crying until I was done.

Nabil Ayers

(author, record label person)

When I was a child in New York City, my mother and my uncle used to take me to the World Trade Center the same way parents in other cities took their kids to the zoo or a sporting event. It was always a special outing that was inexpensive and accessible. My stomach dropped every time the elevator shot me up 110 stories, then I'd stand outside on the roof (you used to be able to do that) in awe, as my mother and uncle pointed toward far away neighborhoods in Brooklyn and Queens where our ancestors once lived, and to Long Island where my grandparents lived at the time.

The Twin Towers' skeletal, unfinished frames served as the backdrop of my mother's pregnancy photos, and to me, the towers stood as an iconic representation of New York City. They hid between blocks, magically appearing as landmarks when I needed direction. They watched over the city where I was born, and where several generations of my family had been raised.

I lived in Seattle in my twenties, and although I often traveled to New York, I never visited the World Trade Center as an adult. On 9/11, I hadn't cried in a long time, and as I watched the news, I felt a sharp heat rising slowly in my throat. As I witnessed the horrific loss, I instinctively tried to push back my tears, but it was already too late. My eyes burned as I thought about my connection to the crumbling buildings on my TV screen.

I visualized the grainy photographs of my family visits to the towers—it never felt more important to dig them up than at that moment—and I stopped resisting the guttural noises and warm liquids that my face expelled. As I wiped my face dry with my shirt-sleeve, I thought about how much I took the Twin Towers for granted, like a forgotten family member—even though I stopped visiting them, I thought they'd be there forever.

Camae Ayewa

*(Black Quantum Futurism theorist, professor, poet,
installation artist, playwright, composer)*

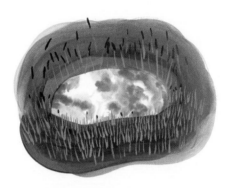

I wouldn't normally identify myself as a crier, but looking at the year 2020 I probably cried the most I have in my life. Everything was sad. I wasn't clear about my path both for my music and my space-time situation, and that uncertainty created within me a sense of despair that felt foreign to me. I must have dropped tears at least three to five times a day, which meant I was a watery mess and couldn't take on any extra emotional stress. And, if you remember 2020, it was filled with front-page racism and violence and uprisings on top of viral anxieties, so it felt like I was forever crying. In October 2019, I remember asking the universe for a break from touring; I wanted to reorganize and restructure. When the world actually locked down I felt a bit of release and relief, but when the summer in Philadelphia turned to fall and winter, I had a realization: I didn't want to spend my life in the so-called inner city; I wanted to be next to water and more nature and less city noise.

Once I realized what I needed to move forward, I started to put my intentions toward what I wanted for my life outside of touring and started thinking more about sustainability and letting go of the baggage that I had been holding on to that no longer served me in a positive way. I haven't cried in a while because I haven't needed to. Don't get me wrong: I think crying is a good and healthy thing, and in the midst of all that crying, I was able to create eight albums that year and form connections and new relationships. While crying isn't something I normally do, I think it's beneficial to get in touch with those emotions. But, for me, crying has its own temporality. Like in the misheard lyrics of the Tina Turner song I've been singing wrong all these years: "I don't really wanna cry no more—'cause it's time for letting go."

Samantha Ayson

(creative)

"Sensitivity is your superpower," read a Slack DM a colleague sent me. I responded back, "lol."

Is crying at work normal? I ask myself this question a lot because I cry at work a lot. Maybe Google knows the answer?

Google says it's unprofessional, actually.

I often have to practice how *not* to cry before meetings that I know will reach a minimal threshold of tension. It never works and I end up crying anyway. My superpower is just too strong.

Whenever I cry at work, I'm mostly embarrassed that someone else had to witness *that*. The irony about being hypersensitive is that you mostly experience the world outside of your own body. I'm on Zoom, ugly crying, and I'm thinking about how *you're* feeling.

Call me unprofessional. I'll probably cry about it.

Gelsey Bell

(singer, songwriter, scholar)

It is very hard to sing while crying. Crying can shut a gate on your throat. It can hijack your pitch, crumble your tone, and sap your vocal power. Yet singing can also induce crying, as it opens your physical and emotional vulnerabilities en route to beautiful, embodied music-making. I can't count how many voice lessons I unexpectedly found myself crying in when I was first learning vocal technique. Even now, if I stifle or ignore a need to cry, it will rear its head as I start to warm up my voice and it will not back down until I have met it head-on. Healthy singing is like an emotional lie detector—you must be entirely truthful with yourself to sing openly, vulnerably, without tension. Part of what we train for as singers is how to negotiate crying. How to breathe through what may transform into sobs. How to accept, to love, to nurture whatever the tears are forcing us to reckon with. How to work through them quickly if we need to so that we can still do our jobs. How to ride the wave of opening yourself so that you are simply skimming the tears and then breathing them back into song.

One of my most challenging attempts at tearful control was the closing night of a Broadway show I performed in, *Natasha, Pierre*

& the Great Comet of 1812. At times it felt like every seat in the house was filled with crying audience members. I swear the theater became more humid. You could hear people sobbing sometimes, like scattered animal noises in a forest. And it was contagious. There was one moment where my staging left me dancing in one of the aisles among the audience. During a long-standing ovation, surrounded by the sounds of twelve hundred audience members yelling and clapping and flat-out crying, I hid my face and prayed my microphone was off so that no one could hear me trying to catch my breath through my tears. It was one of the most overwhelming experiences of my life. But when the music started up again, I was right back to smiling and singing . . . with perhaps the slightest tremor.

Matt Berninger

(songwriter, front man of the National)

I'm fifty-two and I cry more now than when I was a kid. Of the grown men I've shared this with, including my dad, most of them have admitted the same thing.

It's a different kind of crying than I remember. I'm sure it has something to do with the series of traumas since 9/11, the passing of friends, and the planet dying—but a lot of good things have happened in the last twenty years, too. It might just be that I'm finally comfortable with myself enough to let it out. I've matured into a crybaby.

My crying is almost never triggered by a specific event (although the Mister Rogers documentary, *Won't You Be My Neighbor?*, was a recent exception). It feels more like an intermittent release of general sadness and anxiety. It can happen anywhere—in cars, on my bike, at the beach, onstage—but it happens most often alone, in the hours before sunrise. This is the best place for it. I've been waking up around 5 a.m. every morning since my thirties. I used to lie there tossing and turning. I almost never fall back to sleep, so I stopped fighting it. I get up, make some tea, smoke a little weed, and look out the window and think about everything. These are good hours.

In that silence, without anything to do or anyone to talk to—when not even birds are paying attention—I can slowly let the tangled knot of emotional wires loosen a little. It always feels like there are two knots at the same time, one in my head and one in my chest. It's easier to get the one in my head to loosen up just enough to be able to pull on some of the strands and see where they go. I never get the knot out, but I can sometimes get a better look at what the mess is. I can write some thoughts down or record them. There are rarely any epiphanies, just little descriptions of wires.

The knot in my chest is harder to loosen. The threads are gooier and hard to get a hold of. I usually don't even bother. But when I do get into it, I usually end up sobbing. I find no relief in just letting it out a little. Tiny, graceful teardrops aren't going to get me anywhere. I grab a roll of paper towels and collapse into it. It's usually over before I know it. A good one can last five full minutes, or they can be as quick as Holly Hunter's in *Broadcast News*.

The knotted wires never go away, but if I ignore them they just grow and tighten and get hotter. Crying all over them is my only option. Afterward, I'm always relieved. Sometimes euphoric.

Leann Bey

(writer, nanny)

As a caretaker of children for over twelve years, the one thing I know for certain about crying is that you can never really understand what has led to another person's need to cry, but it doesn't actually matter.

Crying is a call from within the house. It is always to be taken seriously because it is always serious. It is to be taken as plain as a statement: *I am in need. I am needing.*

Crying is to say "Sound the alarm! There is SOMETHING!!!" Whatever that something is, it is enough of a something for that person. Crying is the alarm.

No one else gets to say how valid or "serious" that something is.

When someone is crying, the only obligation another person has is to offer what they are able to offer in that moment, in hopes that it might be something that is needed.

Sometimes it is, but most times it isn't, but that doesn't actually matter.

What matters is that an offer was extended. An attempt was made to answer the call that's been put forth, reaching out for something, and in extending an offer (of any kind), we are usually able to find connection somewhere in the middle.

Sonya Bilocerkowycz

(writer, educator, author of On Our Way Home from the Revolution*)*

When the Russians started bombing Kyiv, I heard sounds I'd never heard before or since. To be clear: I was far away from Kyiv, far away from the bombing. The sounds came from inside my body.

It is almost midnight on a Wednesday in western New York, and I am trying to drag myself through another hour of work before classes the next morning. I am behind on everything. February has already been a sleepless and shitty month, with tens of thousands of Russian troops breathing down the borders of Ukraine. A few days earlier, Vladimir Putin gave a televised address in which he called Ukrainians "those dearest to us . . . [our] friends . . . [our] relatives, people bound by blood." Putin's jowls looked dusty and inflamed as he spoke.

To an outside observer, such words might suggest affection. To Ukrainians—who have been resisting Russian colonial violence for centuries—they are sinister, nauseating words. Busia, my Ukrainian grandmother, taught me never to trust what the Kremlin said, only what it did. She's been dead several years now, but her wariness is lodged like a concrete block in my stomach. For weeks the dread just sits there, calcifying.

My phone vibrates on the desk.

Sorry friend.

That's the entire message. No preamble, no reference to anything beyond itself. Two simple words of condolence from an American friend.

I blink at the screen. I know what it means.

I move my hands to open a tab and type the first news site I can think of. Explosions in Kyiv. In Kharkiv. Mariupol. Ivano-Frankivsk. Lutsk—a small city near Busia's village, the village where one of our cousins still lives. Missiles are striking every region of Ukraine. The headline font is so large—EXPLOSIONS—the page itself a soundless scream. Russia's full-scale invasion has begun.

I stumble from the desk and toward the bed, cradling my phone like an egg. Something starts to unravel. To spool backward, like a building constructed but in reverse. Concrete collapsing in on itself, crumbling, rubble, dust—*Sorry friend*—spooling, spooling back to the village, to a storks' nest atop a dead tree, stuck like a grassy lollipop into the mouth of the sky, spooling back to the field of rust-colored poppies, to jars of pickled beets, a pig in the yard, the occupiers' plodding boots, the looting, Busia fleeing, her father deported, everyone gone, people bound by blood, *by blood*. EXPLOSIONS.

But I am far away from Kyiv. Far away from the bombing.

Curled over my phone, alight with messages, my chest clatters. A rush of liquid and sound I do not recognize, have never heard before. I wail, and the wailing is alien—or, perhaps, it is ancient. The stone in my stomach cleaves.

It isn't just me, there on the bed, wailing through the bombing. Those tears belong to someone else.

Mike Birbiglia

(writer, comedian, filmmaker)

'm watching the movie *Spotlight* with my wife, Jenny, in our living room.

I'm crying. That kind of crying where if you were in a car in the rain you'd have to pull over. The moment that breaks me is when a man confesses to a reporter in a diner that he was molested by a priest when he was a child. There's something about this scene that is so vivid and real and painful that, after all of the articles I've read and news reports and documentaries about the sexual abuse by Catholic priests, this was the scene that broke me.

I'm crying so hard that I actually have to pause the movie. I cry for fifteen minutes before we turn it back on. I've never cried like this during a movie. Which possibly made Jen think that I was abused as a child. I was an altar boy in Massachusetts, after all. But I wasn't abused, not to my knowledge. There was something about this film and what I've read cumulatively that made me cry for all those kids. Maybe I knew kids who were abused. Maybe I didn't.

When people debate the resurfacing of sexual abuse allegations in entertainment, politics, and other prominent fields, there is often quiet pushback—not made on social media or even in op-eds—where people argue "It was a long time ago."

Maybe that's why *Spotlight* is important.

Those kids who are now adults were abused a long time ago. But it lingers. For the victims, the pain often never goes away. The complicit nature of our culture will continue until we shine a spotlight on these things. To shine a spotlight on what has happened in the past and how we can all be better in the future seems like a noble attempt to step forward. It's a step forward not just for us, but for our children.

I think about this with comedy a lot.

Comedians sometimes get criticized for dark jokes that take on dark topics. But I believe that those jokes shine a light too. We can't fill our days with relentless documentaries about pain and abuse. I mean, we can. I listen to public radio too. But most people simply don't. It would be too much pain to bear. Jokes are a way that we acknowledge the darkness. They allow us to say, "I can see you and I can laugh at you and someday I may defeat you." Just because comedians laugh at the darkness doesn't mean they don't cry too.

Zeba Blay

(author, journalist)

was five years old the first time I ever saw an adult in my life cry. It was 1994, and it was also the first time I had ever seen a movie in a theater. The movie was *The Lion King*, and I remember the moment Mufasa died because as the music swelled and tears fell from my eyes. I looked up and saw what would become a core image, a core memory: Kofi, the "fun" adult with the booming laugh and off-color jokes, the one who always got too drunk at parties, sobbing into his bucket of popcorn.

Outside, I asked Kofi about the tears, and asked him if he was all right. I didn't know adults were allowed to cry. I didn't know that they ever did, at least in real life. He laughed off my questions in the way adults do when they sense that children can see right through them. In the garish fluorescent light of the shopping mall, Kofi suddenly looked like a different person. Realer, somehow. And I remember thinking, perhaps not as eloquently, *This is what art can do*. I remember feeling that somewhere, in stories, was a safe space to just *be*.

I was raised to be a "Strong Black Woman." Which is to say, I was raised to repress. To chew down big feelings into something small, more manageable, easier to hide. This was how my mother was brought up, and her mother before that, and this made me something of a problem child growing up. Because all I did as a young girl was cry, and whimper, and sob, and all the adults in my life did was scream, and yell, and regard me with a kind of pitying exasperation.

It never felt *safe* to cry around my family. If I cried, there had to be some kind of justification for it, one that didn't seem self-indulgent. Because to cry without a sufficient reason would invite all kinds of platitudes, reminders that to cry or be sad was tantamount to being frivolous and weak. *There's no use in crying over spilled milk. Big girls don't cry. Crying never solved anything.*

I think that's why I've always loved going to the movies, *crying* at the movies. Because a movie theater is a vessel, a space that holds big emotions and, more than that, exalts them, welcomes them. I love what a profound communal act it can be, to laugh and scream and cry with other people in the dark. I love how safe it can feel in that space to let go. We don't need a justification for being moved, even if the stories and the people are not technically "real."

I've never felt more powerful than when I cried at the first movie I saw in theaters after staying away all of 2020 due to the pandemic. It was a ridiculous, if entertaining, horror movie about getting old and dying. I can remember how strange it felt to sit in the dark with strangers again, how the communal grief of everything happening in the real world permeated the air, how everyone seemed to laugh a little harder, gasp a little louder. And then in the

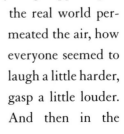

third act, a character who I hadn't expected to die did, and I found myself weeping. And I felt silly, because this was a silly movie, and I couldn't understand it.

And then I heard someone sniffle, and another person sob, and I looked down the row I was seated in, and the row behind me, and the row behind that, and saw several wet faces. And I knew instinctively that this wasn't even really about the movie, that this was something else we were all experiencing. I felt so much power in that moment, a power that seemed to be amplified by the intimate communal act of letting go with other people. Perhaps something small and fragile inside of us broke open, and all we had to do was have the courage to let it.

Caleb Braaten

(founder, Sacred Bones Records)

When's the last time you cried while traveling?
I cry almost every time I fly, and exclusively when I fly. Other forms of travel do not find me nearly as vulnerable.

Since I fly a lot and I cry on nearly every flight it's hard to pin-point the exact last time. But I remember having a good cry while watching one of the worst movies I've ever seen, *Batman v. Superman: Dawn of Justice*.

Why were you crying?
Because their friendship is so complicated!

What are some travel rituals you use to keep your mind in the right place?
I tend to travel light. I will go to great lengths not to check a bag. I always sit in a window seat. I take my shoes off as soon as I sit down. I make sure I have nice headphones, good music, and access to movies.

John Paul Brammer

*(award-winning writer, illustrator,
author of the memoir* ¡Hola Papi!*)*

On a particularly lovely afternoon in Los Angeles, I decided to get myself a treat. I'm not usually in Los Angeles, and I'm not usually in the mood to spoil myself. I got a fine, delicate gold chain from the women's section of a fashionable boutique I sometimes buy from online. I wore it on the long walk back to my hotel with a breeze at my back. It felt correct. I was being swept forward. Everything was going where it was supposed to go. I was going where I needed to be. Briefly, the facts of my life arranged themselves into a legible and exciting constellation.

The next day, the chain was in knots. I'd taken it off and put it down on the table, a small act that was enough to tangle it all up. I picked at it until my fingertips went raw, unable to accept the betrayal of the thing. I was running late for a party. I didn't usually go to parties in the first place. This was an important one, one that was supposed to punctuate a long and difficult journey. I was supposed to meet and drink with important writers. I had made it as an author. I had escaped the place where I grew up in defiance. The minutes crept by. I began to bleed. I refused to go out without wearing the chain, untangled. I hadn't cried in years.

Phoebe Bridgers

(musician, writer)

Crying has always been infuriatingly elusive to me. I remember when my mom told me my grandmother had died. I was nine. I wanted to cry. I wanted to communicate that I understood, that I was deep. I wanted my mom to remember how much I cried when I asked if I could skip the funeral and go to the Harry Potter–themed hot lunch at my school. But it was all I could do not to laugh. I settled on furrowing my brows and nodding like I imagined very intense, introspective people did, and hoped it would read as me bottling up my feelings and staying strong.

The internet tells me that my episodes of nervous laughter could be symptoms of a mild form of Tourette's. I think to myself, "Don't laugh. It is literally the least appropriate time on earth to laugh," but sometimes I just can't hold it back. I laughed when the girl dies in *Bridge to Terabithia*. I laughed when I broke up with my first boyfriend and saw him cry for the first time. I have held my face in my hands at funerals, hoping no one is looking too closely while I try and pass off stifled laughter as sobs.

I went to a performing arts high school in Los Angeles, kind of like *Fame* but with more drugs. People smoked weed and sometimes heroin in the bathrooms and gave each other stick-and-poke tattoos with eyeliner. I let a girl shave half my head in a bathroom once. I saw my English teacher at a Dinosaur Jr. show, and again at a Joyce Manor show. I saw a different English teacher shred lead guitar with his band at the Grove. My math teacher wrote a rap verse on the board every day, and spent at least fifty-five percent of class deconstructing it with us. Reminds me of someone's romanticized idea of art college, but high school.

Mr. Howell was my history teacher. He was different, almost normal. He wore a sweater vest every day, and gave lectures accompanied by meticulous PowerPoint presentations which he never deviated from in all the years he taught there. The closest thing was maybe when he made us watch *Dances with Wolves*, his favorite movie. I'm not sure what the historical relevance was there. His ordinariness was completely out of place at my high school. One day he announced he was going to start working part-time, meaning he would stop teaching our class at the end of the semester. Rumors spread that his wife was sick, and he needed the time off to take care of her.

I was a horrible student. I ditched school so often that it felt safer to not even bother going to class because I'd draw too much attention to myself. Mr. Howell's class was pretty safe though. He didn't know everyone's names, so I'd occasionally go to his class and sneak some highly fraudulent homework onto his desk.

One particular Friday I decided to brave it. Fridays were tough.

Less structured than a normal day at my school, classes started at ten, and we had half-hour periods of all six of our academic classes. The second half of the day was an art elective we only attended on Fridays: hip-hop history, gospel, experimental film, etc. So every half-hour academic period was pretty much total chaos. No one could focus and the teachers didn't care.

On this Friday, Mr. Howell's class was relatively calm, until we had five minutes left. It was his last day teaching, and everyone started talking, and Mr. Howell just gave up and started packing up his desk. When it was time to let us out, he muttered under his breath, while no one listened except for me, who caught it for some reason, "Guess I'll see you guys around." Something in my head said "Don't cry"—and I fucking lost it. I sobbed into my hands and all over my clothes. Everyone stopped talking to stare at me. No one had any idea why I was crying, including Mr. Howell, who came over to me and said, "It's going to be okay," and I snotted all over his sweater vest.

Anna Bulbrook

(musician, idea doula, prose enthusiast, cofounder of Metalabel, founder of Gxrlschool, curator for TED)

I dreaded movie day in middle school because I knew that at any moment during *The Lion King*, I could go from zero to Peak Cry with no transitional time whatsoever. Something sad—or worse, happy—would happen to Simba, and I'd be scrubbing at fat tears with the sleeve of my Abercrombie sweatshirt. Then I'd look around at a sea of classmates who were, impossibly, not sobbing? Did they not feel the same hot, volcanic spillage? What was wrong with me?

This, uh, special ability at crying is both a gift (I feel everything deeply; I have an exquisitely primed release valve) and a pathology (my container spills over far too easily, or maybe I had no container to start with).

Here are some tips on crying from my years of experience:

1. **Cry swagger.** Like nausea, avoiding crying makes it worse. You can't sidestep it, but you *can* own it. Summon some damn swagger.
2. **Towels > tissues.** Tissues sand your face and end up as weird little crumbs in your dryer. Towels are soft, absorbent, *large*,

and washable. They're ergonomically perfect for crying. Always cry into a towel.

3. **Get low; make noise.** If you have privacy, both visual and sonic, I suggest getting low, like all the way down to the floor, but in a ball shape, and MAKING SOME NOISE [air horn]. I like to heave inconsolably for extra catharsis. You can also do this on a dance floor.

4. **Water crying.** Water crying is the sublime act of crying outdoors in rain, mist, or *the ocean*, which is made of tears. It's even better if you are doing something in motion, like running, so you really feel the elements whoosh past. Have you ever emotionally hiked while cold rain pelts your face on a mountaintop? Or sobbed while riding a bicycle through sleet? Or done literally any ocean stuff while weeping? Which leads me to . . .

5. **Shower crying.** If you don't have access to a rainstorm or large body of water, try a shower. Press your forehead against the cool tile and sob while water dramatically sluices down your back. Do this for less than ninety seconds, please, for the environment. Then find a nice towel.

6. **A little help.** Sometimes you need an on-ramp. Make a "cry list" of friends whose love fast-tracks your throat to choking. Listen to a dolorous song like "Song for Zula" by Phosphorescent and watch videos of devoted dogs reuniting with

undeserving humans. Find a large group of people singing in unison and try to sing along. (This one gets me every time.)

7. **Crying in public.** Sometimes, you legally can't have privacy due to being on an airplane or being contractually obligated to be onstage in front of several thousand people. On a plane, find a distant focal point and gaze at it intensely while soft, elegant tears run down your face. Onstage, though, you *can* cry during most moments and people will think it's a touching part of the show. Plus, they're probably crying too.

8. **When not to cry.** Don't cry if you need to sing or say anything audible, or if you can't find a towel.

9. **Have low expectations.** Crying is a sublime release, but let it be what it is. It's not good, not bad, not super fun, and not even a solution most of the time. And yet, most of the time it's all you need.

'Nathan Burgoine

(writer, former bookseller)

I clung to a woman more than twice my age in the bookstore where I worked, both of us crying. I considered her many things: customer, regular, friend, and delight.

I proposed the day after the law changed, and now I was married. Before, if regulars asked me if I had a wife, or was married, I said "No." No lie.

But now?

I prevaricated when they asked. "My better half read that. It's good," instead of "My husband read that. He thought it was good."

No real difference between the two, but out loud the former diminished what the latter declared. It rankled me to adjust my words, but I'd learned to be wary. It wasn't just how straight people mentioned their husbands and wives constantly, but how often they assumed a skinny white guy like me agreed with their bigoted views.

I felt a self-imposed pressure to stay quiet.

The woman recovered from crying faster than I did. No surprise; she was a Polish woman in her late eighties who survived a Germany that lives only in books for me. She was bright and kind to a world that was neither to her. She was my favorite customer at every bookstore I'd worked. She followed me, store to store, as I got promoted. We exchanged Christmas cards, birthday wishes, small tokens of friendship.

And still, I hadn't told her.

But a few moments before the crying, she'd noticed my wedding ring, and said, "Oh! You got married!"

"Yes," I said, and the free fall in my stomach began. Understand: As much as possible with someone you see only monthly, I loved this woman. She was one of the reasons I was a bookseller. It certainly wasn't the pay, or the hours. Customers like her.

"What's your wife's name?" she asked.

And that was it. I respected this woman, I loved my husband, and I wasn't going to lie.

"Husband," I said. "His name is Dan." It came out calm, a bit reserved, and maybe close to a whisper. I braced for her reaction.

She burst into tears.

I hugged her on reflex, startled, and into my ear this wonderful woman whispered, "I'm so happy for you. I was never that brave."

So I held a woman more than twice my age, in the middle of a bookstore, crying. Two people who'd known each other over a decade, whispering words we should have been allowed to shout.

Jane Butler

(great-grandmother, AI gig worker)

I am seventy-three now, though I was just six years old in this photograph taken during my father's funeral at Arlington National
Cemetery in 1954. It has haunted me all these years, for I have no
memory of the event. I recognize myself. Yet the place, the handling
of the folded flag, the sorrow of those in attendance, my tears, are
impossible for me to recall.

Within eight days of the plane crash, the air force arranged our
move from Texas to my grandparents' home in Philadelphia, ordered my family's household to be shipped, and scheduled my father's burial at Arlington. The blizzard of paperwork and news
clippings sit in a box at my feet. The memories from that time frag-
ment into snapshots from before and after this photograph. They
swirl around a somber, crowded house, tables and counters full
of food, the helpful airline stewardess on the flight east. Then my
grandmother's kindness envelops me, the scent of her pantry, picking peppermint leaves for tea in my grandfather's garden, playing
with my mother's childhood dollhouse. Her gentle companionship
cushioned the aftershock of his death.

Our family's annual pilgrimage to Arlington weighed heavily

on me throughout the following years. The waxing and waning of depression was dependably timed, keyed to the arrival of autumn.

It has been thirty-seven years since I last visited Arlington in person. The map displayed on the website is stark, winter-browned grass and leafless trees. I cross the bridge again in my mind's eye, follow the winding road up the hillside to his gravesite. The mourners in the photograph are gone now, swept away by the relentless passage of time.

And I, grown old, have come to accept the necessity and comfort of these forgotten tears; the dissociation between my present self and the experience of the little girl mourning graveside for her beloved father is complete, mercifully unfathomable, tightly bound in a place and a time—Arlington, October 1954.

Mairead Case

(writer, teacher, author of See You in the Morning *and* Tiny)

My mom taught me how not to cry. I don't remember asking to learn. She said it was helpful when it wasn't the right time to show emotion, which I knew meant being the only adult in the room, looking out for your sister, or during emergencies. Here's how: Press the tip of your tongue into the top of your mouth, right where the upper teeth sprout, and look up. You will be physically unable to cry.

For a long time, I never tried it because I rarely cried. I wanted to, but I didn't think I had the time or the liquids. My body and my work had nothing to leak or lose. I rocketed around cities skeletally, heart in hand. Emotions were something that whacked me in the chest while reading or at shows. I do remember sobbing when I left homes (family, boyfriends), but at these times I wanted an animal instinct, a process for existing in a body. Mom's tool didn't help. I did pass along her advice to friends starting hormones. Today, I love the person I was, because if I don't neither of us exist.

Years later, in late winter, my principal said we needed to prepare everyone to go home for a while. There was a virus. I gave books and granola bars to the kids whose home was school, asked my Spanish speakers to teach us what a corona was, and then we all watched a short film about staying in love with someone for a long time, decades more than any of us had yet been alive. Some of those people were lovers. Some were siblings. One of them talked about sex, and the kids who got it laughed.

Afterward we went to the playground. Under the sky, the kids spun and shrieked, and I rode the waves of caring for them and about them. One whose name kept shifting got her hair stuck in the swing chain, and we unstuck it together. When I felt the sobs bloom in my chest, I remembered what Mom said, and finally her advice was helpful. I needed a boundary, so I could be the adult and the kids could be the kids. I clenched my tongue, and I looked up. I thought about how Mom separated herself from me, so she could hold on and then let me go. I didn't cry until I got to the car.

Daniel Chamberlin

(east central Indiana artist, writer)

At emergency medical technician school, they taught us that "your job is caring for people on the worst day of their lives." Going to work as a first responder means bearing witness to the inevitable genesis of suffering. Helping strangers through tears of pain, while their people shake with tears of grief.

We also learned to take care of ourselves first, our partners second, and the patients third: You can't help your patient if you become another patient. Until you're on scene, it's hard to understand that this means repressing empathy. You can't start an IV, hold a C-spine, or administer sternal rubs if you're sobbing on the side of the road.

EMS work meant being present for suffering, but—even with the extended transport times of our remote Far West Texas service— it was a fleeting encounter. We stopped leaks, packaged the patient onto a backboard, and delivered them to a higher level of care. Then back to the station where my veteran paramedic partners would self-soothe with bowls of cereal and *Hogan's Heroes*. "You okay?"

they'd ask, but I was more likely to be offered a
cigarette, a Bible verse, or a gas station corn dog
than a shoulder to cry on.

Being present for others' suffering in a
heightened state of focus can make it easier to
avoid the pain of sitting with your own hurt.
The adrenaline triggered by lights and sirens makes
it easier to focus on questions like "Skull or gray matter?"
when assessing a scalped motorcyclist by headlamp at 2 a.m. After
the adrenaline dissipates, memories remain.

Stoics opt for quiet, self-imposed estrangement. EMTs predis-
posed to stoicism might opt for quiet, self-imposed estrangement.
Trauma junkies prolong their alienation with black humor and
gory tall tales. As a Zen student, I've tried to expand my understanding of suffering into something inclusive that applies to all of
us. It's not the silence or macabre jokes that isolate us. It's the denial
of our shared suffering as witnesses.

American Zen teacher Lewis Richmond expresses* the ubiquity
of human suffering as "you are not alone."

"The fact that we all suffer means we are all in the same boat,"
he continues, "and that's what allows us to feel compassion."

I am grateful for the quiet, elusive connections
formed in blood with my fellow medics.
But as I'm reminded whenever I let my
guard down and allow others to take care
of me, everyone can experience connections
formed in tears.

*Andrew Cooper, "The Authentic Life: A Conversation with Lewis Rich-
mond," *Tricycle*, Summer 2010, tricycle.org/magazine/authentic-life/, accessed
June 21, 2022.

Lauretta Charlton

(writer, editor, The New York Times*)*

There is death, and then there is the cruel, ruthless bodily and cognitive decline that is caused by Alzheimer's disease.

When I finally realized I could no longer speak with my mother, that she was, in some ways, already dead, I cried.

She and I were never close. I always got the impression that she wanted to be somewhere else—someone else. I was hurt by the idea that she perhaps had fantasies of another life in which I did not exist.

Her struggle with the disease started early. She even warned me, "My mother has dementia, and I'm starting to forget things too." Being young and arrogant, I figured by naming the thing she had taken away its power. I was wrong. She was probably more scared and more vulnerable in that moment than she had ever been in her entire life.

And yet I carried on, bitter that we didn't have the sort of mother-daughter relationship I felt we deserved. I carried on not talking to her, telling myself it was for my own good, that there was nothing to say.

When the disease took over, I was in denial. I was still too hurt and confused. I still couldn't bring myself to say the things I wanted to say to her. There's still time, I thought. She's still in there.

Yes, she is still my mother, of course, but she's not there. My mother is somewhere else, as she has always been. I cry when I think of that place, unreachable.

Maybe I, too, will find myself there one day. I'll tell her that I love her.

Leah Clancy

(poet, friend)

Some of us tap into our palm or touch each finger to our thumbs; some of us fling open a closed fist finger by finger, counting out the syllables. I tap mine out on the table next to me like I'm dialing a phone number. Some close their eyes to concentrate, but mine remain open, fixed on some absent middle distance. Five, seven, five—three lines typed out on a typewriter. I finish the haiku, handing it to the person standing before me. And sometimes, when I've done it right, they might just cry.

I've always been a poet, and I've worked with Haikuists for the past six years; it's a company hired to write custom haiku for guests. Weddings, birthday parties, gala fundraisers, company conferences, music festivals—each gig is its own chance to cut straight through the social niceties, to connect with a stranger on any topic of their choosing with a contemporary take on the traditional Japanese poetic form. The subject might be lighthearted or silly, but it frequently gets personal. I've had people tell me they were pregnant before they've told anyone else. I've had people tell me about attempting suicide, about proposing to the love of their life, about moving away to college, having a miscarriage, reconnecting with an old friend, about their biggest dreams, about their worst fears. And dogs. Lots and lots of people's dogs.

It's incredible how quickly people welcome the chance to be *extremely* vulnerable. Most crying experiences happen as the guest receives their haiku—they're overwhelmed by the poem's emotional acuity, tears welling in their eyes, surprised to have their experience echoed so accurately by a stranger. Parents gasp at how perfect poems are about their children, lovers amazed by poems for their other half, individuals in disbelief at how profoundly validating it can feel to read a reflection of themselves. They cry in recognition and revelation, in gratitude and affirmation. This is by no means a testament to my writing, but rather, the power of listening.

Ultimately, Haikuists is a case study proving that all people want is to be seen and heard. Not just noticed— *observed*, considered, made to feel special. "How are you?" is a conversational throat-clearing. But when you're asked what you want your poem to be about, you're given a chance to receive the time, space, and attention you deserve. Each haiku is a memento that assures the guest that their stories and ideas are worthy of being turned into a tiny work of art. And as a poet? It feels bizarrely satisfying, seeing in real time the impact your words can have. When we wrap up the event, we'll ask each other "Did you have anyone cry?," and with an odd pride, we exchange stories of the interactions.

Sometimes the tears start flowing before we even start writing, just as the guest begins to open up, particularly when there's a sadness—rejection, grief, separation, loss. When it comes to trying to seem "normal" or "okay," my friend uses an analogy of holding a beach ball under water: the deeper and longer you push it under, the greater the effort and exhaustion. But in this disarming moment when a stranger says, "Yes, tell me *anything*," you can let that object rise to the surface, a gigantic and relieving release, the poem its buoy. It's an honor to have folks share intimate details so I can write a small tribute to heartbreak, to life, or to love lost. And in these brief seventeen-syllable moments, I might find myself choked up, weeping alongside them.

George Clarke

(musician, photographer, vocalist in Deafheaven)

cried on our bus in Austin, Texas, July 2018 after an anxiety attack. It was the third show of my first tour without drinking. I stopped six months before.

Exercise and cleaning ground me during that tour. If we're in a bus or hotel, there's a quietness in making a bed.

Aliya Cohen

(psychic)

'm a psychic medium and I cry at everything: the media, water, compliments, terror, concerts, relationships, animals, next steps, endings. Onward.

When speaking to others, I am often told I am sweet and kind (they don't know it's a defense mechanism). If I can project enough kindness to the point of someone crying, we've both become safe. Their tears are the proof. The tears are the answer to these questions: Have I pushed them to the top of the cry-o-meter? Have I made a lasting impression, so they will never think anything badly of me? Am I good in their eyes? Did I win? Am *I* safe now?

It's not meant to be a sinister game. It's self-protection, stemming from childhood bullying. It gives me a sense of control. But I tend to overthink everything. I ask: If the effect of an interaction is making someone feel so good, and I only say the good things that I mean, does my intention matter in the first place? I am often unconscious of this mechanism at play and don't always realize I have a choice in the matter. I'm working on that. However, there is one space where I am always conscious of the energy dynamic.

When I am psychically looking at someone, whether it be during a reading, healing, or animal communication, there are no social games. I have no expectations or goals. I don't need feedback if I've given a good reading or not. It's not about me at all. I am reading from a place without judgment or competition or projection, but from a place of complete neutrality. People cry, and it has nothing to do with me. This is immensely liberating.

With the neutrality, it's important that I remain open to the client's emotions, thoughts, or sensations, without going numb or matching their emotions. I can't see them clearly if my own body needs tending to because it has gone un-neutral and is crying now too. Outside of this space I can be more flimsy with my boundaries and become an emotional, teary-eyed mush. But in session, the more neutral I am, the more truth of a soul I see, the more space I give my clients to feel safe.

My clients don't cry when I talk to their loved one who has passed away. They don't cry when they think they could've given their pet the best life possible and didn't, or when they reveal their self-doubts. They cry when they are reassured that their choices don't have to be regrets, and that any worries (anxieties/self-doubts) don't reflect their identity. They cry when they hear that they are more than their traumas; when I validate that they are deserving of real love. They cry when they hear it's okay to take up space, that they can ask for what they need, and that they are already on the path to their dreams. They cry when I remind them that they are such a bright soul who is doing so, so well and that it's all going to be okay.

And they really are doing great. They don't always know that, but I can see it. The energy doesn't lie. They cry when someone else sees the light in them because, for however long, they thought it was gone—or worse, they never knew it was there. They cry when someone else sees the light in them because, finally, they can see it too. I get the honor of seeing them begin the journey of returning to themselves. And, like every journey, there will be some tears along the way.

For all the ways I may people-please in my day-to-day life, sessions have taught me the give-and-take of authenticity between two people. I can only build a safe space to a certain degree; what others show up with is what truly creates a safe environment. So maybe the next time I am brought to tears from catching a proposal in the street or watching my best friend graduate college or seeing the wind in the trees, I can say with certainty, "Thank you for showing up. Thank you for seeing me. Thank you for bringing me home."

Cat Cohen

(comedian, actor, author of God I Feel Modern Tonight*)*

've paid thirteen thousand dollars to inject myself with hormones guaranteed to put me in a bad mood. I'm walking through Central Park crying into an almond croissant. I'm told the follicles will grow until the eggs mature. You can freeze your eggs now and have children later. Will it be romantic? Getting pregnant at the hospital? Remember romance? At the carnival holding Jack's hand? Fuck it. I text Ruby, *What's fun anymore?* Am I doing this because I'm cosmically bored or just thirty years old? Is there a difference?

I decide to freeze my eggs because I'm a career-obsessed whore who might want to have a daughter at age sixty-five. It all felt very casual until I fetched the needles from the pharmacy uptown. My breasts hurt. I wouldn't normally call them that, but I'm being medical right now. You understand. I have to squirt the meds into my belly fat for ten days. For once I'm grateful that my gut billows over low-rise denim.

The whole thing is a bit sci-fi for my taste. It feels like the right thing to do, which means it's not very fun at all. It's quite a racket being a modern woman who doesn't know what she wants. The

hormones have sent me into "egg mode." I'm sobbing all the time—
juicy roast-beef tears pool in my ducts.

Just a few more days until the retrieval. Time is heavy. I read
books about young people, their bruises; old people, their regrets.
Everything I say is ambient noise. I'm wear-
ing a poplin dress and googling *maudlin*
(I always forget what it means). I don't
need to explain it to you. How it burns
good in the palms. The slow coming
on of a sadness about nothing and
everything all at once.

I mope and swell underground, saying
nothing excites me anymore. I have a dream that I love famous people. "I just love them lately!" I proclaim in the streets. In my waking
life, I'm a clogged faucet. Growing eggs I don't know if I'll need.
Bloated and lonely at Soho House, where a guy introduces himself
as "Chase. Like the bank." My moods egg and flow. I ride the wave.

Jamie Coletta

(a mom, wife, music publicist, human who can't stop crying)

I marked it down.

I cried six times in the last week. First, there was the drive to the veterinarian with my senior dog. As the A/C blew cold air in her face, I choked up thinking about how many more times we'd realistically make that drive together. There was a tough-night-of-toddler-parenting cry, a moving-into-a-new-office-and-overwhelmed-by-junk cry, and a few hormonal cries, for good measure.

Crying has always been a part of who I am. It happens often and easily; I can bring myself to tears at a moment's notice. Give me sixty seconds and I can get myself there. Intrusive thoughts are just chillin' at the gates; all I have to do is let one in.

It's made pretty much any form of vulnerability, positive or negative, extremely challenging for me. I used to ask my therapist all the time—what's wrong with me that it's so easy for me to cry? Sometimes I can't even get a sentence out before it starts. He reminded me that it's possible to have an overactive amygdala, a.k.a. the emotional center of the brain. He told me that children who lived in a constant fight-or-flight environment are bound to have some lingering PTSD; of course, until they're ready to deal with it in therapy.

I'm sure an influencer would tell me to make it my superpower. Maybe it is. But I'm still working on accepting this part of my-self. I probably always will.

Or maybe I should just start a band called Overactive Amygdala instead.

Randolph Cornelius

(Professor Emeritus of Psychological Science, Vassar College, whose lifelong passion has been the study of crying)

A little over three weeks ago [August 14, 2004], at the final Phish concert in Coventry, Vermont, Trey Anastasio, the lead guitarist and singer of the band, began sobbing while talking to the audience in the middle of the band's penultimate set. For someone who was ending a twenty-one-year relationship with the other members of his band, reflecting on his experiences and the music he and his bandmates had made in front of thousands of adoring fans at his band's last concert, such an emotional display might be expected. In fact, it would have been odd for Mr. Anastasio to not be deeply moved on the occasion and so his tears are quite unremarkable. While few of us have sobbed in front of seventy thousand people, and even though there is tremendous variability in the propensity of people to cry, most of us as adults have cried at some point in front of other people. Such emotional displays happen often enough that they may be considered mundane. The lyrics of a couple of popular songs to the contrary, everyone—or almost everyone—cries. I would like to argue, however, that Mr. Anastasio's tears—and yours and mine—are anything but mundane when examined from the perspective of the science of emotion. They are, rather, quite extraordinary, and are quite extraordinarily complex and interesting. They can tell us much, I believe, about what it means to be human.

A tear seems like such a simple thing. By volume, it is little more than what you get out of a gentle squeeze of an eyedropper. Composed of water, various proteins, enzymes, lipids, a little potassium and manganese, the hormone prolactin, and some secretory immunoglobulin A, emotional tears are produced by the same glands in the corners of the eyes that excrete the tear fluid that keeps the cornea moist and, because it contains an antibacterial enzyme called lysozyme, defends the surface of the eyes against infection. All terrestrial animals produce tears that moisten and protect the eye but—and here is the first extraordinary thing about crying—only humans produce tears in response to emotional stimuli. Although Pliny the Elder reported that crocodiles shed tears when they eat their prey and Charles Darwin described a female elephant in the London Zoological Gardens who wept copious tears when separated from her calf, as far as modern science has been able to demonstrate, humans are the only animals that cry. Now, this is not to say that other animals do not show signs of distress when they are suffering or utter alarm calls or cry out in pain. This they most certainly do, and crying has been regarded by some as related to the distress calls of other animals. Only humans, however, possess this particular form of emotional display. Mark Twain once said that human beings were the only animals that blushed . . . or needed to. Are human beings the only animals that need to cry? I'm not sure if there's an answer to that question, but I can certainly tell you something about *why* humans cry.

I began my studies of crying twenty-five years ago with the research that formed the basis of my doctoral dissertation. I had no idea at the time that attempting to simply describe crying precisely and then to discern some of its meanings would consume most of my career as a researcher. I did realize almost immediately, however, that I was onto something of considerable significance, most certainly to the participants in my research. I asked a simple question, "Please tell me about the last time you cried in front of another person," and got in return a collection of intensely remembered, sometimes harrowing accounts of life at its extremes that often left me, at the end of the day, in tears myself.

One young woman told me of the day when she—barely nineteen at the time with a six-month-old infant in her arms—gave her permission for her husband's life support, who was in the final stages of a long battle with cancer and who had suffered cardiac arrest, to be withdrawn. She spoke of the tears that waited until the papers were signed, then dampened the shoulders of the surgical gown of a nurse whose name she never knew. A young man in his thirties, a veteran who had had half of his face shot away during a firefight in Vietnam, who lost an eye and gained a metal plate to replace the portions of his skull that were shattered, spoke of a breakthrough in the psychotherapy he had sought to deal with the many memories that tormented him. He described the call he had made to his therapist intending to leave a message informing her that he was committing suicide. She answered the phone instead and was able to use his desperation to get through to him. He told me of the moment when he felt hot tears begin to roll down his cheeks. "What's weird, man," he said, "is that the tears came from both of my eyes and I know I only have one." Another young man told me of how his ex-wife had driven his beloved dog, a dog he had had since he was a teenager, to a remote spot in the Sonoran Desert in Mexico and released it there without food or water to die of starvation or dehydration. He said she was gleeful when she called to tell him that she had done this. "How could anyone be so cruel to a dog?!" he tearfully asked me.

Each of these stories, and those
of many of the other participants,
involved individuals struggling
against situations that had become overwhelming to them,
situations in which their ability
to cope was exhausted. In addition to great sadness and grief, the
participants in my samples reported
feeling helpless, powerless, and extremely
vulnerable when they cried. There was obviously a pattern regarding the kinds of emotions
often associated with crying, but another pattern was apparent to
me as well. The situations described by the participants, at a some-
what more abstract level, were all about the same thing, namely,
what the psychologist John Bowlby called attachment, which can be
best characterized as an enduring emotional bond between people.
Bowlby studied the attachment relationship between mother and
infant, but attachment is a useful concept for describing what goes
on between adults as well. In examining my data, I quickly came to
realize that crying seemed to occur most frequently in situations in
which bonds of attachment had been broken or were in danger of
being broken.

Now, this may not seem like such an earth-shattering realization, but this pattern, or metapattern as [Gregory] Bateson might
call it, had considerable predictive utility that helped me make sense
of something that I, and a number of students of crying before me,
had no small difficulty understanding. If crying is all about feeling
helpless and vulnerable and not being able to cope, then why do we
cry when we're happy? Earlier researchers had attempted to explain
happy tears by arguing that when we cry out of happiness what

we're really crying about is how unhappy we were previously. This explanation never made any sense to me. As it so happens, I had asked some of the people I interviewed for my dissertation work to tell me about a situation in which they had cried out of happiness. The situations they described turned out to be about attachment as well, but instead of attachment bonds being broken, they were about attachment bonds being reestablished, as when one greets a family member or loved one who has been away, or reaffirmed, as when old friends shed a tear over a fond memory they share.

An examination of the vast array of situations in which we shed emotional tears reveals that, while there are exceptions—sometimes we cry just because our nervous system needs to get back to a lower state of arousal, as Darwin recognized—most are indeed about attachment. There is a lovely poem by Jorge Luis Borges, "Matthew XXV:30," that describes—in his wise, achingly evocative voice, which comes through even in translation—some of these situations:

> *love, and the imminence of love, and intolerable remembering.*
> *dreams like buried treasure, generous luck*
> *and memory itself, where a glance can make men dizzy—*

Tellingly, perhaps, Borges's poem is a commentary on the Parable of the Talents in the book of Matthew in the Bible. As quoted by Borges, the parable ends with the lines:

> *And cast ye the unprofitable servant into outer darkness:*
> *There shall be weeping and gnashing of teeth.*

I'll leave it to you to decide if the unprofitable servant's reaction to his fate fits the attachment model of crying.

Elizabeth Cronin

(florist, founder of Asrai Garden)

Each evening, as I drove toward my home during the last few months of my marriage, I was filled with dread about what would greet me when I walked through the door.

I would turn left on Forty-Seventh Street and, instead of parking out front, drive past my house. I would reach

for my phone, put on "Storms" by Fleetwood Mac, and just drive . . . through the train yards, around the neighborhood, around the park.

What usually started as soft, calm crying would work its way into a guttural sob as Stevie sang "and not all the prayers in the world can save us." I pressed repeat on the track over and over and over and over. And, when I finally stopped crying, I headed back to my home, parked the car, wiped my face, and tried to find the words to say what I knew I needed to say, tried to summon the strength to allow the possibility of my happiness to be greater than my fear.

Then, one day in September—not particularly different from any other day—I parked the car, walked inside, and found the courage to actually leave. When he asked me if I could stay, if we could work it out, I reminded him that each time over the past two years when he had lashed out, punched the wall, said something awful, treated me terribly, I told him, "You are doing irreparable harm to us." Me finally leaving was what I meant by irreparable; our marriage was impossible to rectify or repair.

When I finally said what I needed to say, I did not shed one fucking tear.

Sloane Crosley

(author of two novels and three books of essays,
cofounder of Sad Stuff on the Street *[the website],*
editor of Sad Stuff on the Street *[the book])*

I cry so much, you could salt pasta water with the tears on my cheeks. I do it regularly, with both joy and sorrow, at the sight of certain mementos or videos, but the most *vivid* instances involve witnesses. Crying opens a portal of awkwardness in other people. No one knows how to handle how fast you've reached the edge, especially if you are, for the most part, an even-keeled person. When someone bursts into hysterics, it highlights how little we understand the emotional range of others. Several years ago, I was sleeping with a man shortly after the sudden death of my best friend. I knocked my head against his wall and this moderate pain unlocked something both extreme and embarrassing. I don't think I've cried that hard before or since, in front of anyone, and I hated him a little in that moment, for being there to witness it, for patting me on the head.

But my sharpest and earliest memory of a witness to unmitigated tears came after hearing the Joan Baez song "February." I was in middle school and some local sadist must've put it on a mixtape. The song is about a couple whose relationship falls apart. Over

Christmas, they give each other presents but no cards. Ouch. By the time spring comes and the buds push up through the ground, our heroine is so devoid of romantic feeling, she has no idea what the fuck flowers are. She takes a walk with her lover and he points out a crocus and she asks, "What's a crocus?" "It's a flower," he explains. Then she asks: "What's a flower?" My mind was *awash* with despair. I went into my mother's room, presuming a generational familiarity with Joan Baez. But she had never heard this song. So I played it for her, putting headphones over her ears while I offered DVD-style commentary ("She forgets what *flowers* are!!") and cried anew. My mother diagnosed the song as "maudlin." But she could see it was stirring something profound in her young daughter. She hugged me tightly, trying not to laugh, trying to assure me that these things happen in love. Sometimes they're worth it and sometimes they're not, but this too shall pass. Better than a pat on the head, I suppose.

Lilly Dancyger

(author of First Love *and* Negative Space*, former bartender)*

Behind the bar, my job isn't just pouring drinks—it's making every night feel like a party. If everyone is having fun they'll stay longer and buy more drinks and tip better, so I laugh at obnoxious jokes and yell "Shots!" and turn the music up when a good song comes on. I diffuse fights at the pool table and promise "Next one's on me" whenever someone orders a supposedly last drink. I wear short shorts and a push-up bra and demonstrate how to have a good time. It's my job to make it believable that there's nowhere else I'd rather be—even when I just got dumped and I really want to be at home in my pajamas, eating takeout in the dark.

I've gotten good at this divide: I can be sullen on the inside, dancing and cracking jokes on the outside. Sometimes I vent to a few regulars who like to feel like insiders—who don't realize that by complaining to them about bad tippers and jerks, I'm showing them the version of me that will appeal to them most; just like the party-girl version appeals to other customers. But these are just quick asides. Mostly, I am the life of the party.

Until he walks in; the reason I'd rather be home in my sweats. He's a regular, and his friends are regulars, and he can't stop coming

to this bar without admitting that he did something wrong. So he orders a beer like we
weren't just on my roof, talking about
the future, a few short weeks ago.
Like he didn't tell me stories about
his childhood and sigh about how
he never wanted to leave my bed,
touching my face as if memorizing
it. I pour his beer and set it in front
of him like he's anyone else, just a customer, playing along. Then I go to the
walk-in to restock some bottles.

I don't realize how loud the bar is until I'm inside the quiet of
the walk-in—a dank, dimly lit little hovel with low, dripping ceil-
ings and a sloping floor. The cold air stings my nostrils as the heavy
door clicks shut behind me. Here, I don't have to be any version of
me; I can stand still, close my eyes, feel the goose bumps rising on
my arms. I can double over with one jagged sob, contort my face,
and silently scream. I can shake with tears and cold all at once. But
just for a few seconds—no longer than it could reasonably take to
find the beer I'm looking for. And then I dab under my eyes to fix
my smeared mascara, roll my shoulders back, exhale a plume of hot
breath into the icy air, grab a six-pack, and get back behind the bar.
Back to being the life of the party.

Jon DeRosa

(vocalist/guitarist of Aarktica, somatic practitioner)

I have grown to be in awe of the power of tears and the story they tell. Often while working with a somatic client, a single tear (usually from the left eye) is released without their conscious awareness and signifies an "opening." It indicates that this person is moving through resistance and entering a deep place, one where there is potential for profound healing. I sometimes refer to it as the "time machine," because they are going back in time to the point of trauma and feeling in the body the emotion as it was felt then. This is different than playing it back from memory, which is not as reliable as the body's account. From here, they can acknowledge the words unsaid that need to be said, the emotions unexpressed that have been longing to be expressed.

With these words and emotions can come all different kinds of physical releases, shakes and tremors from deep in the muscles, or a flood of tears, as if held back by a dam of resistance. They can encapsulate an impossible combination of joy, sorrow, frustration, pain, relief, and so many other emotions that make us the beautiful and complex creatures we are. It is in these places of openness and vulnerability where I have seen the deepest healings occur.

During my own somatic training, I received a particularly deep session from my most trusted teacher. As I entered the "time machine," I found myself in a black void with a hint of light in the distance above me, as if I had fallen downward through a long well or tunnel. As I got my bearings, I realized I had arrived at the moment of my own physical embodiment, the instant my soul entered my body, presumably while still in the womb. I could "feel" and "see" the light of the "Source" above me, and the memory of "Home" was vivid for me, in the same way one can recall the childhood home they grew up in. I grasped upward, sobbing uncontrollably because, in that moment, I was so confused, so afraid to be abandoned in this unfamiliar place, away from "Home" with no idea how to survive. I howled and cried from the depth of my being as a small child would, "I want to go back, I want to go back."

This trauma of the spirit being embodied but "unwilling" is one I carried into this life, and is one I expect to process for a long time. It was a religious experience that reminds me of the complex relationship between the physical and the nonphysical, and how we delicately move through this life as humans piecing together the mystery of who we are and where we come from.

Madi Diaz

(musician, songwriter, avid crier;
wrote a song called "Crying in Public")

My plan was to make it through airport security. My plan was to make it through airport security and down the long terminal hallways, onto and off of the moving walkways, and to my gate. If I could make it to my gate, then maybe I could make it onto the plane, all the way down the aisle to my middle-row seat, and maybe if I made it to my seat, I would make it into the air, back onto the ground and OFF the plane, and somehow make it into a cab and up the stairs and on the other side of my own front door. Yes. My plan was to hold it DOWN and make it all the way back to MY home where everything smelled and looked and felt and was familiar.

But it came in spite of me. I had no part in it. I was just some human vessel of sad shit stumbling through the metal detector robot-portal thingy, trying to put my shoes back on at the other end of the luggage belt. I was crying. And I decided it felt good and I let it feel good. I let all of what I had planned to contain pour out of me and left a trail of it from security to Terminal C for Crying. JK, I can hardly remember what city I was even in. That's a lie, I remember exactly what city I was in and exactly what happened where, with who, when, and never why, but that's not the important part. I sat down against a wall in a dull pile and let the crying take over and didn't feel anything else for a minute. I felt people walking past and somehow didn't leave my body to be one of them, to look at myself, which was probably the only reason I didn't stop crying. I don't remember time passing. I don't remember moving, breathing, thinking fast or slow. I felt humming and meditative.

When I came back up there was a note sitting on top of my suitcase. I can half remember someone putting it there. I can half remember looking into someone's eyes only briefly, but directly. I read the note, I stood up, and I got on the plane. An older man next to me shared a baseball game streaming on his laptop. He told me he had a kid my age. I got home, put my bags down, and I hung the note on my refrigerator. I kept it for years and years. I've moved so many times since that it was lost somewhere in the shuffle, but I remember that it said at the bottom: *"I hope you can remember that we are human, there is love."* So I guess this is kinda my note to you. When you come back up, there is love.

Sadie Dupuis

(musician, poet, writer)

One Site Posts to the Other

It's not cathartic crying on an exercise machine
just a bright migraine I self-induce.

Bees in the gag now. Snotting into escrow.

Each day my face is unrecognizable to me
making it hard to establish a cosmetic practice.

Tried to get into myself so much I locked me out.
      Beautified, a draconian tag that needs to get low.

      I die by the record and un-die.
      If the DJ plays my song I crown them queen.

      If the DJ spots me in the crowd they know before I do
      whether my mask is really this scary.

Elia Einhorn

*(radio host, musician who releases under
the moniker Fashion Brigade)*

Patrick's a crier," my producer, Les, mentioned as she prepped me for my interview with Patrick Haggerty, the man behind the pioneering queer country-music act Lavender Country. "Ah, I don't cry much these days," I responded absentmindedly, reviewing my notes one last time before the seventy-seven-year-old singer joined our Zoom. Within half an hour, tears were streaming down my face as Patrick recounted the story of how, back when he was a boy in rural Washington in the fifties, his farmer father let him wear a beautiful dress and makeup to sing in his school's talent show. Afterward, his dad's only feedback was sharing a few tips on how to improve the performance for next time. I was crying for little Patrick, a boy who had no idea yet what he was up against in life as a gay person; for my own father, gone three years now, who in the mid-nineties told his nail-polish-wearing teenage son that if I was gay, it was okay; and for myself, a dad to a young daughter that my wife and I have raised to be proud and self-assured, whoever she turns out to be. "Man, I can't stop crying!" I said to Patrick as he finished the story. "You *should* cry!" he responded, sobbing anew. And he was right.

Valerie Ettenhofer

(pop culture critic)

In movies, characters often say that it's hard to cry after loss. When I lost four loved ones in just over a year beginning in December 2019, I found out that the lesson that's baked into so many great stories simply wasn't true for me.

I'm a pop culture critic, and I'm honored to spend my time identifying the stories that make me feel more connected to the world, and that I think may move others in the same way as well. Emotional response is far from the only valuable metric used to evaluate art, but in 2021, walled in by the isolating claustrophobia of grief, that became a moot point. Everything I watched made me cry.

I cried watching shows that elicited tears by design, like the therapy-intensive second season of *Ted Lasso* or Russell T. Davies's beautiful portrait of queer youth amid the rise of AIDS, *It's a Sin*. But I also spilled tears over media that it didn't even make sense to cry about, bawling my way through YouTube yoga videos and sniffling over dream sequences from *The Sopranos*. Still, despite all the tears, I felt stuck in my emotions. No matter how touching the art, nothing seemed able to stop my grief from feeling both endless and lonely. Until I watched a movie about Nicolas Cage and a pig.

When I saw Michael Sarnoski's *Pig* in theaters, I expected to see a *John Wick*–style revenge thriller. Instead, what I found was a profound meditation on the tactile realities of grief. The film follows a widower and former chef named Robin who has lost his trusty truffle pig. Robin spends much of the movie bloodied and dirt-caked, his pain turned external and unignorable. He clings to his loss so hard that it leaves marks on him. But little by little, throughout the movie, he loosens his grip on grief, instead reaching for good food, and memories, and other people.

Sometime during *Pig*'s third act, I started sniffling. Then the person next to me did too. Then the person next to them. Eventually, all three of us began to audibly cry, our sounds encouraging one another and layering like a small orchestra of emotions. Afterward, I met both criers in the bathroom, and we laughed about our shared moment. I saw their grief-stained faces, and they saw mine. For the first time in months, I felt better.

Jessica Garcia Fox

(survivor advocate)

I never thought this day would come," Ruth whispered to me as she waited to give her testimony to the jury.

As a survivor advocate, I am no stranger to tears. When I met Ruth, she had just escaped her abuser. She had lived through so much trauma. She had survived human trafficking, sexual assault, and exploitation over the span of a decade.

I remember picking her up when she escaped. She ran to my car with nothing but the clothes on her back and a black trash bag full of the few possessions she had left. She was sobbing as we drove away. You could see the fear in her eyes. She cried so much that she could barely catch her breath. I remember her asking: *"What if he finds me? What if he tracks me down? What if I don't make it out of this alive?"*

But today was different. Ruth, as brave and resilient as ever, was taking a stand against the man who had hurt her. After speaking her truth to the jury, we returned to my office and nervously awaited the jury's decision on whether her abuser would spend the next thirty years in prison for the crimes he had committed against her. After hours of waiting, we finally got the verdict: guilty.

Ruth turned toward me, her eyes once again welling up with tears. But this time for another reason. Her face had softened. As she smiled, her tears began to fall. I did not see fear or anxiety. I saw relief. I saw light. I saw someone who finally felt safe again. I'll always remember what she said to me before leaving that day:

"I did it. I survived."

Grashina Gabelmann

(editor-in-chief and cofounder of Flaneur *magazine,*
writer, translator)

don't remember who I said it to or what prompted it. It's one of those memories that is more a memory of a memory than a memory itself, but I remember proudly telling a kid in elementary school that I hadn't cried at school all year. I've told this anecdote to a couple of therapists to illustrate my emotionally closed-off upbringing. Another hazy memory around the same time is of my mother telling me coldly to stop crying. She used the German word *heulen* for crying, which really doesn't translate into English. The word is harsh and contains, at least to my ears, an immediate judgment—it implies that crying is for wusses. I felt there wasn't space to cry at home and my sister felt the same. She reckons our parents didn't know how to regulate emotions and therefore couldn't teach us how to either. If you see your kid cry and don't know how to deal with it, the easiest solution must be to tell them to stop.

I remember being on the phone with my sister's godfather, who had just returned to Canada from visiting us in Germany. I missed him so terribly I couldn't open my mouth to speak because I knew doing so would cause me to bawl, so I just communicated via nods.

My mother, sitting next to me, laughed and told me, "He can't see your nods over the phone." I can still recall the burning pain in my chest and throat from the pushed-down tears.

Not really being allowed to cry was especially tricky for a kid who moved to a different country every three years or so. When I was nine, we moved from Germany to Canada. I was so sad to leave my best friend but all I could do was pace and stare at the ground instead of looking her in the eyes and saying goodbye. If I spoke, I was afraid my voice would start to quiver, and I knew tears closely follow quivers.

I was thirteen when we left Canada. I ensured the departure would be less painful by finding everything in Canada horrible. I sabotaged my last months there to avoid tears, but when we arrived in Denmark, the suppressed emotions caught up with me in the form of rebellion and I was nearly expelled.

I eventually reconnected to crying some years after moving out. Now I cry in public, on my own, in front of partners and friends. It feels so good—maybe because it was forbidden for so long. Yesterday I texted someone: *I'm so sad I'm actually crying right now.* I want people to know I'm crying because, according to my logic, it means I'm not coldhearted like I used to believe I was. I haven't yet cried in front of my mother, and I've never seen her cry. I don't know if I'll be able to. I still find it scary to be emotionally vulnerable with her, but every tear I cry is a tear she wasn't able to release.

Tavi Gevinson

(actor, writer, founder of Rookie *magazine)*

Crying is sort of evil to me as an actor because it is often thought to signify that a character is deep, that a performance is "real," or that a scene has become "serious," and that, therefore, a play is truthful. Crying usually feels or appears to me like merely a symbolic gesture, which is ironic considering how it's used to indicate to the audience that *life* is taking place.

If I sound judgmental of actors who choose crying, it's only because I've been that actor and I'm still embarrassed that I was ever that actor. I thought that because the character I was playing was in an impossible situation, forced to make impossible decisions under impossible pressure, she would cry. A lot. I was able to do it onstage by inhaling through my nose and cutting off the breath to invoke a yawn and make my eyes water. Sometimes I dabbed vegetable glycerin in my eyes before going onstage. But there are so many other things people do when they are suffering: steel themselves, shut down, try *not* to cry. Halfway through the run of this play, a member of the creative team watched it again for the first time in months, found me backstage after, and said, "You weren't supposed to cry! The director liked the way you did it on day one of rehearsal!

How you just sat there and looked strong and like you were taking everything in. As soon as you cry, the play is over, because then we know you'll lose." I instantly burst into tears. She then said, "Actors always cry when I tell them that *they're enough*."

Maybe crying in a scene is a way to prove to yourself—even more than to the audience—that you know what you're doing and are good at it; that you've "gotten *there*" or are really "feeling *it*." The more I do plays, the more convinced I am that there is no *there* or *it*. There are only people in a room and a mix of voluntary actions with involuntary feelings. That's what's nice about a live show, and about crying: they're beyond our control.

Sophia Giovannitti

(artist, author of Working Girl)

There's a scene in *Gossip Girl* where Blair tells Chuck she doesn't love him anymore, and they both cry. At least, they both have tears in their eyes; everyone's definition of crying is a little different, often attuned to the frequency with which one does it. Nevertheless, their eyes are glassy, voices slightly choked. I watch this scene a lot on YouTube. I feel connected to Chuck, because I too have had that said to me, and it's a terrible thing to say. You would only say "I don't love you anymore" if you are saying it to someone who still loves you.

When my ex-boyfriend said it to me, we were on a park bench. I cried. A few months later I wrote an essay about the ordeal, and I compared how I felt to someone in a Leonard Cohen song: *You held on to me like I was a crucifix.* I held on to him like he was a crucifix. Where before there was a man, now there was a symbol, and that symbol was so anguished as to be pure, dark, nothing.

A few months before my ex said it to me, Leonard Cohen died. Knowing what that would mean to me, he texted me, and we ended up getting a drink that night, toasting the dead. He did still love me then, though we were already exes, and had been for some time.

And he even loved me still when he said he didn't, and I know that because he told me so after the fact, a year later. Probably most people who say it still love the person; you don't really have to say it if you don't, because reality is obvious in other ways. That's neither here nor there, though. Cohen writes, "The duty of lovers is to tarnish the golden rule."

I don't love you anymore. That's the thing I would say to someone if I wanted to make them cry. But I've never said it to anyone, because it's never been true.

John Gleason

(songwriter, elementary school librarian,
performs in Roadside Graves and Lowlight)

1.

I worked for an educational testing company while I was earning my teaching degree. One winter, they shipped me off to Virginia Beach for two weeks to supervise a cohort of people who were grading open-ended responses on state tests. It wasn't interesting work, but I was young and excited to be working away from home. One afternoon my boss, an older woman who rarely spoke to me, asked me to drive her back to the hotel after work. As soon as she sat in my car, a horrid-looking red nineties Toyota Corolla I had recently bought for $500, I realized something was wrong. Something beyond a bad or tiring workday. She sat in silence, so I played the CD I had already loaded that morning, Tom Waits's *Small Change*. "Tom Traubert's Blues" is the opening track. It's a weighty song. Quite possibly one of his finest compositions and devastatingly beautiful. She started crying midway through the song, looking straight ahead at the highway. As the song ended, we arrived at the hotel. She finally looked my way and said, "Thank you. I needed that."

2.

I walked into the school, and my colleague abruptly came up to me to say, "You look really tired!"

I replied, "I was crying in my car" and walked away.

(It was the two-year mark of my mother's death from cancer.)

3.

Once in our school library a student was crying in the corner. I asked him what was wrong and he held up *Bartholomew and the Oobleck* by Dr. Seuss and sobbed loudly, "This book has too many words!"

(He was right. It has 2,898 words as compared to *Cat in the Hat*, which only has 1,626.)

4.

My father died under hospice care in my aunt's house. I was fortunate to witness his final days. My mother, who had been divorced from my father for quite some time, walked into his room one night alone and closed the door. I could hear her crying through the wall, telling my father things maybe I shouldn't have heard. They were all good things, great things. Things that maybe should have been said years before. Healing things. (Shit, I'm crying now.) He died later that night in his sleep.

5.

There's a live performance of Fleetwood Mac playing "Landslide" where Stevie Nicks quietly touches Lindsey Buckingham's shoulder as he plays his guitar. When I first saw this, I cried. I wish I could tell you why. It seems so ridiculous now, but not at that moment.

Pia Glenn

(actor, singer, writer, dancer, always has gum in her bag)

A full beat. That's what I was trained to call it. In this case, the beat refers to neither music nor violence, but a face of glam makeup, labored over and perfected until the bearer is ready to hit the stage, runway, party, or, simply, their fabulous life.

I often say I'm a glamorous Tarzan, raised in the wild by drag queens. This was back when makeup techniques like highlighting and baking were still considered trade secrets, as opposed to the topic of every third TikTok.

Under the most sparkly of tutelage, and as a glittery diversion from Young Pia's difficult home situation, I honed makeup techniques that I'd use when I made my Broadway debut at twenty-two. As a lead. Hair flip.

Unless you're paying a personal makeup artist by blowing your own *Real Housewives*–level money (Beverly Hills, not Potomac), you do your own makeup on Broadway. And crying in full beat is a crisis that must be contained.

YOU MUST PRESERVE THE BEAT.

Simply by virtue of the amount of time spent in show mode, eight shows a week, even the most hardened show-must-go-on mentality will succumb at some point to the body's physiological response. You will experience sadness, and you will produce tears.

The first goal is to stop tears from falling at all: You tilt your head upward and create a small reservoir under each eye, using a folded tissue, paper towel, bit of fabric from your costume—whatever's handy—to absorb the tears. Make sure to hold the absorber of choice perpendicular to your face—never press against it.

If tears must fall, tilt your head back even farther, aiming to have the tears fall from the corners of your eyes, straight down toward the ears. That line is a highly blendable beat border that can be patched up with greater ease than the front of the face. (Be mindful not to let the tears fall into your ears. Giving yourself swimmer's ear during tear management would be too embarrassing.)

So you're holding your head up and back, like you have a nosebleed. Except the tissues are at your temples, and it's your heart that's bleeding. If need be, enlist another person to hold Q-tips at the inner corners of your eyes while you hold the tissues on the sides. Remember, it's okay to ask for help in preserving the beat.

And it's always "preserve the beat." Not "don't cry." Your sadness over [X HEARTACHE AND/OR TRAGIC LOSS] doesn't care that you're doing a show. So, cry your heart out. But maintain that mug and be ready to enter stage left for the cheerful finale when you hear your cue.

By the way, the more cheerful the number following a crying episode, the more unhinged you will become. You don't know true suffering until you've fought back tears while doing an enthusiastic time step for a cheering crowd, everyone on their feet as confetti cannons go off.

But that beat? Intact, hunny. Take a bow.

Sam Goblin

(mental health worker, musician with Mister Goblin)

On a shitty, rainy October evening at the height of the pandemic I ventured to the drive-in to catch some movie I now can't even recall the name of. We showed up a quarter of the way through the preceding film, which was Pixar's *Coco*, and within twenty minutes I was crying so hard that we had to leave.

As a musician in my pretend life and a mental health worker in my real one, I spend my fair share of time around waterworks. While I'm generally pro-crying, it should be noted that it isn't always helpful. As the only species who uses it for anything more than eyeball lubrication, crying is the most uniquely human tool we have to facilitate connection. It's a flare we throw when we can't find our own way out of the woods; an air-raid siren for healthy attachment. When we cry to draw people in and it works, we experience a positive mood shift. When we cry to draw people in and we're ignored or invalidated, we tend to feel markedly worse. Luckily, those who were with me at the drive-in were sympathetic enough to help me get the fuck out of there before *Coco* devastated me beyond repair.

In my work, there's usually very little I can do to alter the material conditions causing the client in my office to sob. Most of what

I can do is bear witness and make them feel comfortable and understood, reflecting back to them what they've found upsetting and lending them my (hopefully) calmer nervous system.

Songs have a similar ability to keep us company in the experience of a specific feeling, maybe even better than people do. No therapist in the world could make me feel understood in the way Nina Nastasia's "The Matter (of Our Discussion)" does, for example. Songs that  look you in the eye have the power to attenuate shame, guilt, despair, or any of the other flavors of misery more effectively than the most potent SSRI on the market. It's not uncommon that I'll be talking to someone in music and when I tell them about my mental health work they say, "That's cool, I wish I did something that was actually helpful." I would argue that those who make music are doing something more helpful, more therapeutic than most clinicians—you just may not know who you're doing it for. For all you know, you could be sitting with a stranger right now, one hand on the small of their back as they blow mucus into your sleeve.

Sarah Faith Gottesdiener

(author, artist, facilitator, the Moon Studio)

Tears are beautiful because they are an interruption. A reminder that we are water-filled, more porous than we might like, and, sometimes, we leak. They remind us that we are connected to a greater world—one filled with wonder and also heartbreak—while our unruly inside waves come pouring out. Tears are healing because they release stress and tension.

It's a shame that tears have been synonymous with weakness, because it's a shame that we are taught to hold our pain, shame, joy, and wonder inside. It's a shame we aren't meant to have interruptions. It's a shame we aren't meant to show how, on the inside, we're all filled to the brim. Memes of men crying spread like wildfire, another reminder that our society wants us to be hard machines, never pausing, never allowed to be fully seen. Tears are misconstrued as weakness because we are often vulnerable when we cry: torn from the whirl of productivity by this water, the need to be cared for, the need to be witnessed. We must pause, we must rest, we must process, we must tend.

As someone who has held space for thousands of people's tears, I'm not afraid of them. It's usually an everyday occurrence, maybe

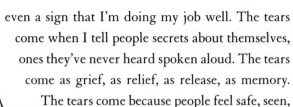

even a sign that I'm doing my job well. The tears come when I tell people secrets about themselves, ones they've never heard spoken aloud. The tears come as grief, as relief, as release, as memory. The tears come because people feel safe, seen, heard, and affirmed. I welcome the clear tracks streaming across their open faces, and marvel at our natural, physiological alchemy. If I were president, we'd have state-funded grieving parties. Where people could cry for hours and be witnessed and held with love.

Sasha Grey

(actor, writer, musician, content creator)

We are born crying, the fluid from our mother's womb expelled from our lungs as we take our first breath. It's how we communicate before we can speak. When we get older, crying can make us feel incredibly helpless, like a young child. My last good cry was recent; I was slightly curled on the couch, all of my limbs squeezing in toward my chest. This should paint a picture for you that these were sad tears; it's rare to experience sad tears while in a perfect posture. I waited until the end of the night to release them; I'd been holding in my pain all day so I wouldn't lose myself and become unproductive. It was the anniversary of my father's death, and I've approached my grief this way over the past few years. Because I know exactly how I will feel that day, I can actively control my tears. It's a relief. The sneakier bouts of emotions that arise usually come with the change of the seasons, in the days leading up to this anniversary. This is when I can't control the tears, and these emotions can be overwhelming. I'll smell a sweet flower or a hint of a cigarette, and it reminds me of spending the summer with my dad.

As I laid there, I realized that crying is the one response to our emotions that mirror what it was like in the womb. We often close our bodies inward, like fetuses, enveloped by tears and runny noses. In these moments we may even lose our- selves in an unconscious attempt to release our- selves from anguish. We are at our most vul- nerable. I found myself feeling exactly as I did when I was a kid, desiring to be held or comforted by my parents. I remembered that one day my mom will depart this earth and the sinking feeling became deeper. Then a flash of my dad crying happy tears entered my mind, the faint echo of his wheezing uncontrollable laughter rang in my ear, and everything seemed alright.

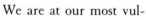

Craig Grossi

(writer, speaker, Marine, author of Craig & Fred *and* Second Chances*)*

I was on an ice rink in Millersville, Pennsylvania, thousands of miles away from the desert, the darkness, and the war I left behind, when I finally broke down.

It started with an odd man rush up center ice. My linemate had ricocheted the puck off the boards just before his body was blind-sided by the enemy. As I took a few strides through the neutral zone, I felt the familiar anxiety of many pairs of eyes upon me, eyes that wanted to kill. It was a feeling I knew intimately from my time in Helmand Province of Afghanistan.

I crossed the opposing team's blue line and, out of the corner of my eye, saw a hulking shape heave toward me, like a dump truck barreling through an intersection. With no time, or God-given ability to make a move, I put my shoulder down and leaned in, protecting the puck with my body. To my surprise the dump truck was made of cardboard. It caved under the force of my shoulder, clamoring to the ice. But more were in pursuit, and I had to keep moving.

I looked ahead and saw my lane to the goal. With a few more strides, I closed in on my target. Staring right through its padded occupant—he was an insignificant obstacle—I took my shot.

I felt my team surround me, punching me with joy. The puck lay in the back of the net and my heart filled with something more than glory. It was a sense of relief that I was right where I belonged.

Playing hockey might seem like a stark contrast from the life of a Marine in combat, but for me, it was the closest I had come to feeling alive since facing death. For years post-deployment I had struggled to find that feeling again—a sense of purpose that comes with the shared burden of a hopeless war. I'd taken job after job and drank beer after beer, each time coming up empty. The only people I'd ever cared to impress had come home and moved on—some of their paths led to more deployments, some to new careers and families, and for too many others, suicide. My search for a meaningful life was starting to feel hopeless.

As a last-ditch effort, I enrolled in college courses. On a dare to myself I tried out for Georgetown University's hockey team. I made the cut. I was thirty years old, with a full beard and a jockstrap older than my teammates. But it didn't matter. Something was alive in me again. Something I hadn't felt since pulling my fellow Marines up a muddy canal bank in a Taliban-infested river valley. Putting one foot in front of the other, for one another. Mud, blood, and smiles plastered on our faces.

Against the glass that day, on the ice, I broke down in tears. I made my way to the bench and collapsed. My teammates turned their focus to the resuming game. It was the first goal of the first game of our season, statistically insignificant. Emotionally, however, it was devastating. It felt like surviving a firefight, knowing that another one was just moments away.

I sat on the bench, sobbing. Each thump of my

heart produced more and more, reminding me that tears and blood are both indicators of a life well lived.

For now, on a rink in the middle of nowhere, I had found my place, and with a team that valued what I had to offer. Four years after coming back from war, I was finally home.

Pepper Hart

(writer, actor)

Lately, I haven't been crying as much as before. Although, I cried with joy while I was in Disneyland with my daughter. At first, I thought I was crying because I had overcome so much and brought my kid there myself. Then, as I was going on rides and eating candy, I realized it was my inner child weeping from deep within because it was relieved I'd finally made it there.

I have had many good cries, but none like that. I often cry when the plane leaves home. My house is near the airport. In a window seat, I end up watching my neighborhood become so small. I feel like I'm running away. I usually mask my face and take the time to let some tears roll out where I am safe and not alone.

I have read books by powerful women I admire, and they always seem to address crying. They recommend just doing it, because it will come out anyway. I don't envy anyone who was forced to not cry as a child. My mom did it to me when I was a teen and it made some serious rage build up, where I could have just been given a blanket and ice cream.

Becca Harvey

(musician, performs as girlpuppy)

As soon as I opened Google Docs to start writing this, I switched back to Spotify to turn on my playlist called "crying playlist." I'm currently stuffed inside a Sprinter van with six other people on the way to Chicago to play a show. As a singer-songwriter, I find myself crying a lot. Music has always made me cry. I think the first song I ever cried to was "My Little Girl" by Tim McGraw, which is a song my dad introduced me to when I was seven. Most of my tears come from songs about parents or children. I think I forget how much I love my parents until I hear people sing about theirs.

I can cry anytime or anywhere, and most of the time it comes without even realizing I'm about to cry. I'm a Pisces, so I blame it on that. I started crying the most when I moved out of my parents' house. Anytime I'm in my bedroom alone, or in the kitchen alone, or watching TV alone, it's almost guaranteed that something will make me cry. It's difficult for me to cry around other people though, which is why I reserve it for anytime I'm alone. I could maybe name three people I can comfortably cry in front of. I'm not ashamed of crying, but I physically cannot cry around certain people. Even as I listen to my crying playlist in the van, which includes at least one song that will always make me cry, I cannot bring myself to show any emotions. As I've gotten older, vulnerability has become more and more difficult for me. The only time I'm comfortable with being vulnerable is with my music.

But I love crying. It's the best thing I can do for myself. I love  the feeling I get in my throat, I love the way it makes my eyes burn, and I especially love the sleep I get afterward. I'll often go out of my way to find something to make me cry, just to feel it again, if I haven't done it in a while. Lately, I've been lying in bed right before I go to sleep, watching TikToks of babies hearing their mom's voices for the first time, or people being reunited with their pets after thinking they've gone missing. Or I'll just put on "marjorie" by Taylor Swift, experience the best sleep of my life, wake up, and do it all again the next night.

Kristin Hayter

(singer, composer, performs as Lingua Ignota)

I have seen footage of the great coloratura soprano Sumi Jo singing Schubert's "Ave Maria" in Paris instead of burying her father in Japan. "I want to be there, but instead I am here to sing for you," she says in French, her breath shallow and heaving with grief. She dedicates the song to her father and her audience waits in agony as the piano accompaniment uncoils. She sings without error, without a trace of anguish or strain in her voice. Her phrases are perfectly supported by breath, absolute and unwavering self-control, decades of training. She is sublime. The body does not have room for both the sob and the "Ave Maria." One must choose: What will hold your pain?

Many times I have cried with a pain that is so vile and unnamable my pores themselves weep and I sweat cold, and I shake and beg God to release me. This feeling leaves me with an ache that cuts and catches at the base of my throat, and so I sing. I veer from the precision and clarity of the grieving Sumi Jo. My voice is grotesque, crackling with snot, wretched, an awful thing. When I am performing, it is my duty to be a vessel, to be empty so that I can hold you. We share the dark together and I reach out to you. I reach out to you with my wet hands and my wet voice and I stand among you, unhinged and unmoored. As I pass between you my lantern catches your face, though you came to see and not to be seen, and the room is a prism of broken hearts, 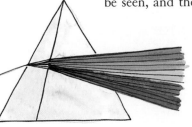 yours as much as mine, and I *see* you. Sometimes I hear a wail, deadened by the sea of bodies. Sometimes a body gives way and falls, the sound of the skin is unmistakable, and we stop and hold you until you can rise again. "Are you   okay?" I ask into the darkness, and the answer is always a meek yes, but the answer is also always an unspeakable no. No, we are not okay. That's why we're here: wailing, falling. Have you begged God to release you lately? Is the pain so bad your skin is weeping? Are you coming to the show? What will hold your pain? Schubert's "Ave Maria" sung perfectly by a woman who would rather be burying her father. A body falling in a dark room. An awful voice sweating and cracking, begging God: *Release me.*

Shelby Hinte

(writer, teacher, associate editor of Write or Die Magazine, *wannabe dirtbag runner)*

'm out on the trail again, though I don't particularly want to be. Less than one mile in and I can already feel tears building up behind my eyes. The sound of my breath echoing in the hood of my coat is one surround-sound lung screaming *I can't do this.* This is a bad sign. I don't remember the last time I went out for a run and wanted to turn back this early. I'm climbing up Mount Madonna and it's pouring rain. A storm came in overnight and the weather feels violent. I didn't pack the proper gear and I'm in a down jacket that is already heavy with rain and pasted to my body. I planned on being on the trail for two hours. I was excited for the challenge of a new trail and rain. The actuality of it is proving to be torture. I know this is mostly in my head, this certainty that I can't go on, that climbing up a mountain in the rain is too hard to do. Impossible. I know this because I have done it before. Loads of times. The only difference is that today I've woken up in a piss-poor mood and I am struggling to get out of it, struggling to convince myself I am capable, that this isn't so bad, that it's enjoyable. I tell myself I will just hit a mile and turn back down the mountain toward the car. A mile in the rain isn't so bad. I can do that. This is a trick of the brain, something I learned when I got sober—breaking time up into smaller chunks so the enormity of the future doesn't crush me. When I was younger, the fear of pain used to paralyze me. Any hint of it and all I could see was the endless infinity of it. When it came to fight or flight, I always chose flight. I hadn't yet heard someone in a twelve-step meeting say *This too shall pass*, and so the present moment always rang eternal.

When my watch chimes, telling me I've gone a mile, I stutter-step, almost turning back for the car, but there is something inside me that is pulling me forward, up the mountain, even though my brain is begging me to give up. This is when the tears come. My mind and body at war with one another. I scream into the rain. "Fuck." And then, "Fuck it." And then, "Okay." I keep going. I keep thinking I will turn back early. I don't. Eventually I get over my bad attitude and the run isn't such a sufferfest. It becomes bearable, fun even, proof that the only way out is through.

I didn't always used to be this dedicated to physical activity. I lacked raw talent. I lacked discipline. I lacked desire. Despite all my lacking, I had a stepfather who was adamant I be involved in sports. This was in large part, I think, because I was chubby. My nicknames at home were "Rolls" and "Chubbo." He often pinched my gut so hard it left little round marks in the folds of my skin. Him and my mother both spent hours in the gym weightlifting and they lived on egg whites and protein shakes. Being fat in our house was the worst type of sin.

When my stepfather wasn't working, or weightlifting, or inflicting pain on my mother, he was racing cars or terrorizing me and my brother. One of his lesser acts of terror was forcing me to be an athlete (though I doubt you can call much of what I did real athleticism). Go-kart racing. Soccer. Basketball. I participated in them because he made me, but I also did them because I thought success in any might make it easier for him to love me. I never arrived at the results I hoped for. Instead, I spent most of my adolescent athletic career in tears: crying at practice because the coaches were frustrated with my lack of coordination, crying before a game in anxiety of my impending failure, crying during the game as my stepfather yelled at me from the sidelines, and crying after when I had to face everyone I disappointed. My stepfather stood on the sidelines screaming curses at me, screaming curses at god, screaming in a way that made him appear like an utter psychopath—arms flailing, spit spraying, hat throwing, hair tugging. I learned to avoid looking in his direction.

That ought to have been the end of my athletic endeavors, but in ninth grade I was sent to live with my father. After years of living with a violent man, followed by years of instability after my mother finally left him, this change was a relief. I was grateful to live in a house where I wasn't afraid to go to sleep at night or open my bedroom door in the morning to whatever chaos might be waiting for me on the other side. Still, I was a teenager in a new town. For months I had only one friend. So, when she joined track and field in the spring, I joined too.

By that time, I was no longer the chubby kid. My soft middle had spread out across my body, and I was nearing six feet. When I walked onto the track for the first practice, the coach's eyes gleamed with visions of my potential, but her dreams fell apart once she put me in front of the hurdles and found that, instead of fearlessly hoisting myself over them, I closed my eyes, squealed, and veered in the opposite direction. She struggled to find another place for me on the team. I couldn't sprint. I wasn't coordinated enough for field events. My long jump was pathetic. With nowhere else to put me, she assigned me the two-miler—an afterthought in track and field.

In my first race I finished a whole three minutes after the other runners. No one on the team would look at me after, not even my friend. I'd made little progress in practice, since I spent most of practice trying to go unnoticed and I often hid in the locker room on what the team referred to as "puke days." I didn't see a point in choosing to put my body through pain when life itself felt plenty painful. I had no interest in showing my capacity for suffering.

Two weeks later, when the gun went off at the start of the second race that season, my performance was even worse. I was barely on my third lap around the track when the other girls began passing me. I don't remember how hard I was pumping my arms and legs, but back then it was my heart that got in the way. I could feel it in my ears and behind my eyes—the pounding of it a dangerous thing threatening to explode. I feared that the pain of running two miles would become unbearable, would knock me to the ground, so the only part of me that moved fast was my heart, racing with the possibility of real agony. When, at the sixth lap, I saw the two front runners were moving in on me and would likely pass me a second time before the race was over, I made a turn off the track at the gate and kept running until I hit the locker room. As if running didn't hurt bad enough, the thought of that level of public mortification felt like an unendurable shame. I ducked into a bathroom stall, sat on the toilet with my face in my palms, and submitted to sobs.

My coach, a peroxide blonde in a visor who never put down her clipboard, came barreling in after me.

"What the fuck just happened out there?" she screamed through the door, though she could hardly be surprised. I mumbled something about throwing up, though I hadn't puked, and even if I had, she'd have preferred I did it on the track than in the bathroom.

It's strange to think that the girl being screamed at in that locker room would ever grow up to become a runner. I rediscovered it on my own terms in my late twenties, when no one was yelling at me in disappointment. This is to say, I was finally able to run when the stakes were low. When I didn't have anything to prove to anyone but myself. Now, I have a daily running practice, I have placed in a handful of races, I have completed an ultra-distance, and I'm toying with the idea of running even farther.

Maybe most notably, I seek out suffering. As a recovering addict, I spent half my life doing the exact opposite—avoiding pain through substances, which wasn't so very different from running away from the track and hiding in the bathroom stalls midrace. Like I said, life is painful enough, so why go chasing more? Why not anesthetize yourself from feeling instead?

When I quit using drugs and alcohol, it turned out my propensity to avoid discomfort was harder to combat than any substance I'd ever been addicted to. I remember attending twelve-step meetings and women telling me it was okay if I cried constantly now that I no longer had the soft barrier of drugs between me and my emotions. They shared stories about their own early days and how they spent weeks uncontrollably sobbing. But I wasn't crying. In fact, I couldn't remember the last time I had cried. As an adult, I'd tried hard not to be the blubbering mess I'd been as an adolescent, crying at the first onset of discomfort. I didn't like crying in front of others. Didn't like how it invited despair in and how, once it entered, there was always the chance it wouldn't ever go away. Suffering begets more suffering. Though maybe that's not the worst thing in the world. Maybe it's attempting to avoid the unavoidable that makes suffering truly miserable.

In ultrarunning, they say most of the anguish stems from thinking about the miles to come and imagining that whatever discomfort you might be experiencing will only grow until it becomes something impossible to overcome. In recovery circles, the phrase "one day at a time" is often given as advice for reducing craving. The idea is that you don't think about the obsession of alcohol as an infinite, never-ending experience. Instead, you try to stay in the present moment. You don't have to worry about never using again, or all the hardship you might endure, or all the ways you might fuck it up. All you have to do is not use right now. Similar advice is given to long-distance runners for races. If you feel like quitting, tell yourself you'll go just another mile, or just around the corner, or just to the next aid station. If you still want to quit when you get there, then quit, but don't quit now. Usually, the discomfort passes. It becomes something bearable.

When I was training for my first marathon, I heard variations of the same advice: *Don't train as if you can escape hurt. Part of training is learning how to cope with the fact that it's going to hurt.* This was a new concept to me. I thought training was supposed to make running long distances less painful, but the truth is, training is about learning how to be in acceptance of pain without any expectation of it dissipating. For a long time, I felt like the ache of life was an impossible thing with which to coexist. I waited and waited for it to end. But like running, life isn't pain-free. Running, pushing myself to go farther or go harder, has become a practice at being better at accepting the suffering in the everyday.

I welcome tears on the trail because they usually arrive as I overcome something I was certain I could not overcome. I cry because I think I cannot stand the pain, think there is no way to continue on; yet somehow, I do.

C. Mavourneen Hogan

(works at Planned Parenthood)

I met a ghost once, working at the clinic. She told me she was a ghost. I was a counselor then, and the ghost made me cry in front of all my patients.

It was almost December. The ghost didn't wear a jacket. She wore a short dress. She wore tall boots with tall heels and no underwear.

We—me and other members of the staff—cried there every day. We cried in the break room and the counseling rooms, and sometimes we had to put calls on hold to cry in the front office. I cried on my first day there, reading the training manual on how to use fetal remains as DNA evidence against rapists in court. We usually didn't cry in recovery, although sorrow and relief hung humid there. And never during the procedure, even when we held hands so hard the nails cut in. That was where we needed to be the strongest.

The ghost told me she didn't want to be there. *No one wanted to be there.* She told me that she had used pliers to uncurl the hook of a metal hanger. She thought she could open her cervix and get the blood out by herself. She didn't know about the pills. She pointed at the plastic anatomical model on the desk, to show me where it hadn't worked.

"I'm not afraid of dying," the ghost laughed. "I'm already dead."

We tried as hard as we could. Do ghosts feel the cold when it's almost December? Do their tall heels slip on the ice? *I'm not doing enough. It will never be enough.*

Afterward, I walked with the ghost to the back door. She held her boots in one arm. Blood ran down her legs and pooled in the paper shoe covers that kept her bare feet from touching the snow. She squeezed my arm with her freezing hand and grinned. She wished me a happy Thanksgiving.

I held my breath until the door closed behind her. I turned to the waiting room full of my patients, and I started to cry. I cried and cried until a nurse came to get me. We went into the counseling room, and the nurse cried too, because she knew that she had also just met a ghost.

Sean Hooks

(writer, college professor)

Having worked with college students since 2002 and teaching a good number of first-year composition classes, I find an interesting form of crying to be that of the "achiever" student. I can tell this student has literally never gotten anything lower than an A- or ninety-something before, not ever in life, and upon receiving that first B- or C there is a level of unstemmed tear flow that I often think of as "this is what it would be like if someone made it until their late teens before they determined that the Tooth Fairy or Santa Claus wasn't real." There's a plaintive and unvarnished "I've been betrayed by my parents and teachers and an entire system of presupposition I've taken for granted," and it also has an "Is this whole life thing just a big simulation?" quality, an "Am I a clone?" quality, or a "He's cut, he's cut, the Russian's cut . . . He's not a machine, he's a man!" quality (from *Rocky IV*, for those of you who might not be connoisseurs of Sly Stallone's litany of sequels).

The consistency and repetition has been eye-opening for me. And while I am a bit of a "tough grader" (high standards are a *good* thing, America; we're seeing far too often these days what happens when you lower them—or have none), there's no sadism or schadenfreude in it on my end, no glee in the alphabetical symbol I've scried atop their paper eliciting such a soundless yet lachrymose response. I do find it an intriguing subcategory of crying—quite distinct from other types I've experienced.

There's no contagious element, other students don't follow suit. They're not funeral tears or crocodile tears. They're not my-favorite-character-just-got-murdered tears or my-kid-just-made-the-game-winning-shot tears. They're certainly nothing like the tears that are reserved for ecstatic joy or excruciating sorrow.

The tears of an adult being chided or scolded by an older adult or authority; yes, there's something of that to it, but these aren't workplace tears or ticketed-by-a-cop tears or wrecked-romance tears. They are the tears of the (almost always first-semester) college student, the frosh, one who tends to be living in a dorm, not a commuter or part-timer. They occur during student conferences, not in a stolen before-or-after-class moment with their teacher. No, this is Who They Are that you've called to task for underperforming—the grade-A getter, gold-star achiever, high-GPA maintainer—and their identity has been cage-rattled, and the tear flow that follows surprises them as much as it does me.

Hua Hsu

(writer, author of Stay True*)*

A few days after the 2016 election, I wandered into a church near where I live and took a seat in one of the back pews. I didn't grow up going to church—I often joke that church was one of the few things my open-minded, mellow parents were intolerant about—and I'm not a particularly religious person. They passed out small pieces of paper with the lyrics not of a hymn but of John Lennon and Yoko Ono's "Imagine." This was not the type of church where people came for the music. Yet we sang, tentatively at first, as though we could not believe these words in this space. We were singing of "no heaven" and dreaming of "no religion,

too" inside a house of worship. It was like an admission that faith was inadequate. All we had was one another, these imperfect voices coming together in a song that had become so ubiquitous and overused that it had been evacuated of all meaning for me. "Imagine" is a song I've heard millions of times. We rarely bother scrutinizing its silly, deeply radical lyrics, its vantage point, the possibility that someone wrote those words because they actually believed them. I sang along with a room of strangers, and we looked at one another, and, for the first time in months, I began to cry.

Joselia Rebekah Hughes

(writer, multidisciplinary artist; she lives with an orange cat, Elliot T. Cat, and is an avid puzzler)

In a town where the sun doesn't set until midnight approaches, a baby is born in the back room of a general store. The back room—peopled by the mother, a midwife, and the storekeeper—is filled with cries. A long shriek of relief. Tears of wonder. Tears of alarm. Missing from the chorus of cries is the baby's young warble. The baby, en caul, rests on the torso of the mother. The midwife looks toward the mother with asking eyes. *Are you ready for the next delivery?* The mother nods her head slowly, never letting her gaze veer from the veiled body of the child. The midwife uses her pinky finger to poke the sac until it tears. Amniotic fluid runs down the mother's hips. Everyone in the room holds their breath as the baby, skin now exposed, fills its lungs with air and emits a wail.

In one version of this story, all four hundred residents of this little dark town, like hungry birds to a newly filled bird feeder, leave their homes and hobbies and other preoccupations to shuffle and run and roll toward the sound extending from the general store. When they arrive, they wait around the building and enact a force field of human energy. They take a deep breath and remain quiet until the baby, who's been wailing off and on for at least ten minutes, settles into its first post-birth sleep. The storekeeper leaves the back room to alert everyone that the baby's at rest.

The townspeople take another deep, collective breath and emit soft chuckles. The chuckling transforms quickly into joyous crying. The crying, unconcerned with narrative clarity, transfigures again and again, meets as many animated registers of expression as the townspeople have lived to experience. The townspeople cry until the sun rises or the baby wakes.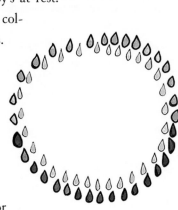

In this version, the townspeople consider communal crying the first gift to all newborns. This gift offers the reassurance that our tearfulness is, indeed, a fullness. With this fullness, we are given our first principles: yes, we are welcome; no, we are not alone.

Aditi Juneja

(changemaker who's working to live joyfully)

I've found that there are two annoying things about having long acrylic nails: it's harder to pick your nose and typing on your phone is challenging. This is a new discovery, as I got acrylic nails—for the first time in a decade and the second time ever—after the *Dobbs* decision overturned *Roe*. I needed to remind myself I was in control of my body. I also bought lingerie after the decision to remind myself that my body can be a source of pleasure and joy and connection— that it's not just a political battlefield.

But I didn't cry.

I cried on the phone with my dad almost two weeks later. Sobbing and screaming about what respect looks like. About how fucked up everything is even as I know that with my financial privilege and living in NYC, I'm not even among those most directly impacted. As I reflected in the following days, what was most striking about those tears was how easily they fell and how quickly they came.

By comparison, I don't remember crying once during the Trump years. Despite working on many of the calamities of the Trump presidency—organizing a list of lawyers at major airports after the Muslim ban, supporting communications around a lawsuit after the emergency declaration to build the border wall, coordinating the response of the National Task Force on Election Crises in the period between the 2020 election and the inauguration—I didn't feel, I worked. And, even when I wasn't directly responding to something, I often held space for folks who worked with me. I called friends in other parts of the movement closer to the problem. I answered questions from people who didn't work in politics about what it all meant. I tweeted.

And I did it with pride. I was good at rapid response. Methodical. Focused. Coordinated. I used to tell people who worked with me, "You'll notice your feelings; have them after we're done." But, I never did. Not really. I cried one time when I was overwhelmed and awed that I had a small part to play in what was happening. This was two weeks before the 2018 election—after the last cable TV show covering the topic was done and the last email sent, I burst into tears. Then I went to sleep. I talked about it with some colleagues at work the next day and moved on.

It was only after inauguration in 2021, when the most imminent threat had passed, that I began to feel. I made myself watch Biden's inauguration so I could reassure myself it actually happened. And then I noticed a shift—I was no longer focused. I was exhausted. Disinterested. Angry. Not really giving a fuck. I knew what had occurred over the last four years, the atrocities that befell our country and my fellow Americans, but I didn't feel anything. I think I was mostly burned out. But I didn't really cry.

I don't remember crying until September, when I decided to leave my job. Then, I sobbed. I cried leaving a place where I had grown up as a professional, my first real job after law school. I cried about the people I was leaving behind. But mostly I cried for all the times that I hadn't cried. I began to process the terrible things that had happened to so many people. The complexity of knowing that I wasn't directly impacted by any particular crisis, but also was proximate to crisis after crisis through my work. Reading, anticipating, strategizing, trying to add value. It took three months and leaving the country to begin to feel. To begin to heal. I saw a massage therapist during my month in Colombia who asked me how I'd been living that way, with so much pain in my body.

This cycle of working hard, burnout, and collapse isn't unique to me. It's very common in political work. And it's not a reflection of the organizations where I worked. I was always encouraged to take time, to prioritize work-life balance, and the people around me held space for me, but I didn't know how to let myself feel. It's part of why I started a podcast called *Self Care Sundays* that went for two seasons in 2017 and 2018. Because I knew that doing work in a cycle of burnout and repair wasn't sustainable for myself or for the movements I was part of. There was always another crisis. And ignoring our feelings during them, especially out of guilt for having them when you're not directly impacted, doesn't mean you don't have feelings. It means they come out in other ways—being easily irritated with family and friends, being rude to colleagues, creating false urgency in work because you're so used to being hopped up on adrenaline.

Feeling is still not my first instinct. I look to analyze and strategize and add value first. But I now notice that I'm not feeling in the moment. I let the people around me know that I'm likely to have a delayed reaction. And then I let them know when it hits me. And I let myself cry when it does. Sometimes that looks like getting my nails done and buying lingerie until the tears will fall. It allows more grace, and ultimately resilience, in this work. Starting with myself. I'm still learning how.

Kim Kelly

(*journalist, metalhead, author of* Fight Like Hell:
The Untold History of American Labor*)*

There was nothing special about that night. It was spring, or maybe summer; I was seventeen, or maybe eighteen—there's not much of a difference when you live in rural South Jersey and the rest of the world is only faintly accessible, a distant fantasy that lies somewhere over the river and up the turnpike. If I was lucky, I'd made it through the first half of my shift as a cashier at CVS without being insulted by a customer or side-eyed by my manager, and the ecstatic freedom of my half-hour dinner break arrived without fanfare. My ritual was always the same: I'd get in my car, drive across the highway to the Popeyes next to the Medport Diner, and buy a box of popcorn chicken (no wedges, add a bottle of water). On most nights after work, I ended up at Medport with my friends Kelly and Erica, or maybe Jesse, and whoever else could be coaxed out on a school night to come sit in the diner's comfortingly beige bubble and smoke cheap cigarettes while nursing tiny white mugs of weak black coffee and housing plates of curly fries. Popeyes was merely an amuse-bouche for the night's real sustenance, but I was so drunk on the idea of having my own spending money that each $5 cardboard box of delicious little nugs felt like a step toward something anyway.

Nugs secured, I parked, rolled down the windows on my white Chevy to let in the cool night air, and turned up my stereo. By then, I'd been writing about music for a couple of years and was already accustomed to spending most of my CVS earnings on CDs and metal magazines; I'd done the same with my first job as a dishwasher, and assumed I'd keep doing so forever. Black metal had captured my heart and soul as only something that comes to you at night when you're sad and scared can, and I spent every waking moment I could listening to new albums and devouring magazine articles about all the bands I hoped to see in the flesh some-day. When my mother got sick and I couldn't cry, at home or at the hospital, all the emotions I'd shoved down would come rushing out when I put on Xasthur or Bathory or Cult of Daath. They said— screamed—what I couldn't.

That night, I was listening to Dissection, a Swedish black metal band whose cut-glass melodies and atmospheric, velvety sense of evil caught me on a deeper level than the rawer, more cataclysmic bands that had been dominating my CD player. I preferred their 1993 debut, *The Somberlain*, over their more well-known 1995 follow-up, *Storm of the Light's Bane*, which was a controversial choice informed partially by the fact that I'd lost my *Storm* CD somewhere. Years later, I'd learn enough uncomfortable truths about the band and its founder to take them out of my regular rotation and stop writing about their music, but during that moment, I didn't know anything about satanic rituals or homophobic hate crimes. I just knew how their records made me feel. They made me feel powerful. They made me feel like I wasn't alone.

And as I sat there with grease staining my fingers, my long hair scraped back into a ponytail, and a coarse blue CVS shirt lumpily embracing my torso, I felt myself start to cry. My break was almost over, "Into Infinite Obscurity" had just come on, and it had just dawned on me that, somewhere else in the world, someone else was listening to this album, too, and feeling the exact same way I was. They felt the power, and the beauty, and the illicit thrill and hint of danger. They got the opening to "Black Horizons" stuck in their head too. Even if I was the only metalhead in my grade and had only just gotten brave enough to start sneaking out to shows at the Trocadero and trying to make friends with people in Cannibal Corpse T-shirts and kissing boys with long hair and tattoos and stubbly beards, that didn't mean I was the only one in the world. "The Cold Winds of Nowhere" hadn't been written for me; it had been written for hundreds, thousands, maybe even millions of us. I decided right then and there that I was going to find them.

And, later, I did.

Kinlaw

(choreographer, vocalist, sound artist)

When's the last time you cried while traveling?
About two weeks ago, while driving.

Where was it?
On the highway, Route 28.

Why were you crying?
I had been in an intensive program this summer that was full of a lot of information, and while it was super stimulating, it was also sometimes overwhelming. I think I saw an animal on the side of the road who had been hit by a car, and it made me burst open and cry.

What are some travel rituals you use to keep your mind in the right place?
I need sleep! If I feel like a place might have a shoddy sleeping situation, I bring my own blow-up mattress and bedding. I have a white noise machine that keeps me from waking up to new sounds. I also really limit drinking alcohol, especially when I'm on tour. I feel hungover pretty easily, so I usually drink maté instead of alcohol during

late nights. I tell myself it's okay to take time alone—I used to feel bad about going home early and being antisocial, but not these days.

I find comfort in being quiet and reading while on the road. Podcasts help me stay centered and curious.

Also, talking! I still sometimes misjudge how taxing speech can be on my voice and when my voice feels strained, it throws off a tour. I'll often set up a quiet place to hang with friends after a performance so I don't over-speak, which turns out to be a nice change of pace and makes for quality time together. There's also a voice coach god named Jeff Rolka who has lots of vocal warm-ups and strengthening videos on YouTube that I swear by. They help me feel flexible and artistically focused. Plus, the exercises help me make time for myself before jumping into things that can be a little more chaotic.

René Kladzyk

(writer, journalist, musician who performs as Ziemba, friend)

I've only cried once with a source. Working as a reporter on the U.S.-Mexico border during a pandemic, there have been so many tears. I've witnessed the tears of ICU nurses; migrants marched across the border back into Mexico, unceremoniously expelled from the U.S.; parents of transgender children trying to make sense of the latest hateful legislation. I've hidden my tears during interviews: that time my editor made me interview a bishop after the Texas abortion ban was passed, and I fought the urge to scream "Liar!" at him when he told me he'd take care of the unwanted babies. Instead, tears ran down my cheeks while I said over the phone, "Thank you so much for your time." I've saved tears for later: on a ride-along with the Border Patrol when the agents kept referring to human beings as "bodies" and caught a seventeen-year-old Guatemalan girl who had been sexually trafficked. She didn't cry as they apprehended her, or when they made her take off her belt and shoes, surrender her phone, and sit in the dirt by their van while they talked on their walkies about more "bodies" on the side of the mountain. Instead, I cried when I drove along the border highway back home.

But I only cried openly once, during a Zoom meeting with a

young woman who lost her uncle to COVID-19. He was a trumpet player: "His lungs were so strong!" Just sixty when he died, he seemed like a real character—and reminded me of my uncle who had also recently died. She started to cry as she talked about him: his sense of humor, his favorite emojis, his idiosyncratic personal style. I found myself crying with her.

Sometimes you need to feel permission to cry for someone else's pain, and I did that day. I think crying for and with someone else is an expression of love. It is the most visual indicator of empathy, and a sign of connection or surrender. But, at other times, it can feel like a transgression, if you don't have enough in common with the person, or don't feel like you're peers. As a reporter, I'm often talking to someone who is fundamentally a stranger. For some interviewees, my tears could almost feel like an insult.

I want to be the person who is okay with how big of a crier I am, to not feel bad if I cry in front of someone who might judge me for it. I want to be a spokesperson saying "Hey, this is a healthy release, there's nothing wrong with crying!" But I feel overcome with shame if I cry at the wrong moment, or if tears come bursting out as I'm trying to navigate conflict and can no longer speak. I rushed to get off the phone with the bishop because I could hear the tears in my voice and I didn't want him to. He hadn't earned that doorway into my humanity. I want to say that it's always okay to cry if you feel like it, but I know this world.

Roberto Carlos Lange

(musician, artist, performs as Helado Negro)

There was this moment when I was in Berlin participating in PEOPLE Festival, the festival that the National and Bon Iver put together with the Michelberger Hotel.

Me and a bunch of other musicians were all in a building, Funkhaus, working together. Everybody would perform in these separate rooms in that space. There'd be this long schedule of performers throughout the day, and you didn't entirely know what was going on in some respects. That was part of the beauty of it.

I'd met these musicians, Bert Cools and Indrė Jurgelevičiūtė, from the band Merope. We'd really gotten along and made some music together—they were super-sweet folks. Again, you didn't entirely know what was going on in some respects, but I did know that Merope was going to perform and so I went to see them.

I walked into this large room and they were set up and they were sound-checking. All these other people started filling up the room and I sat pretty far in the corner. I remember I was kind of tired. I'd just finished making my album, *This Is How You Smile*, and then I'd flown to Berlin. Right before that, I had also broken my rib. I was sitting in this room, and in a way, I was exhausted from that week.

So, we're sitting there and Indrė begins to introduce her and Bert, talking about who they are and the music. Indrė was explaining this music, how it's pre-Christian Lithuanian music that talks about the earth and animals and the forest and the lushness of the world. After she said that, she's like: "Now imagine you're in a forest . . ." As soon as she said it, all the lights quickly went dim and turned green, and the band began to sing and play. I was completely caught off guard and as I was listening, I began to weep. I'm not sure where it came from, but I think it was just crying from the experience of this beauty. I think I was crying at the reality that something could be so powerful to just sweep you away into a world that you weren't expecting to go into.

I haven't had that experience many times. I think maybe I have a layer of cynicism for it. People have come up to me and told me that they've had that experience with my music, but it's been hard for me to have that experience.

I don't know if it'll always happen listening to Merope's music. I think it's always circumstance, the environment, the presence, the vulnerability. But, really, music can be so magical. It's a unique chemistry of space and time.

Rose Lazar

(artist, the illustrator of this book)

Here are two stories where I have publicly cried without expecting to:

1.

I come from a long line of blue-eyed people. Out of the five people in my family somehow mine are the least blue. When people have light-colored eyes, they tend to have more sensitivities to things like light or wind. You often end up looking like you have watery, tear-filled eyes. My mom is the champion of having wet-pool blue eyes. You see them and you know you're either about to laugh yourself silly or cry yourself sick. Thankfully, nine times out of ten, it's usually the former.

When I was twelve, I would still go to church with my mom. She liked to sleep in, and the church offered a Saturday evening mass, so we would go to that one. Going to church on Saturday evening around 5:00 p.m. feels less serious than going to church on a Sunday morning—I'm not sure why, but it just does. Which is why on this one Saturday evening my mom and I almost got asked to leave because we couldn't get it together.

I had this insane winter coat that was like a windbreaker made of patches of colored fabric—it was a lot. It made swishy noises because of the material, so it was loud in two ways. I wore it to church and every time I moved you would hear a loud swishy noise in the quiet. It made it hard for my mom to not laugh.

My mom thinks that she can whisper, but it's sort of like her talking as loud as normal but with a raspy lower tone, making it impossible for her to tell you something on the down low. Which is why when she looked up and saw an older woman wearing a beret that looked exactly like my coat she lost her mind. She whisper-shouts to me, "Rose, you want me to grab that hat for you? It matches your coat. Who knew it was possible? I bet I can take her." Mind you, fifteen people turn around. There is no recovering at this point. We are in a house of worship and my mom is now whisper-singing "Raspberry Beret" by Prince, which doesn't even make sense but there is no stopping her. She won't stop singing and mentioning that she could take this old lady if I want the hat to match my coat.

People are getting concerned, but we're trying to hold back laughing out loud and it's causing a scene. The pair of us are now full-on sobbing in church on a Saturday evening. Thankfully it's almost over and I somehow manage to get my mom back on track and as the service ends and we're walking out my mom is still singing "Raspberry Beret" all the way home.

2.

When I was eighteen my dad died. Death is a very tear-filled and sad thing for reasons that are bigger than this essay, and I did my fair share of crying after finding out. He died when he was living overseas, so it felt remote and unreal at the time.

It was the summer and I had been super excited as I had just finished my freshman year of college and moved into my first apartment. I felt adult. And then I didn't because my dad had died. I had had plans and a summer job and now it felt impossible to do those things. But I still had to, and I had to do them while navigating this big, life-changing event that I didn't feel like telling most people about.

One evening when a couple of friends tried to get me to go out, I said okay. I thought I could handle it and I figured there was no way I had to tell anyone. It was a hardcore show in Buffalo, so I thought if anything I could just hide in a corner and maybe feel a sense of community or catharsis from the room.

Once I got there I realized *Nope, I am not cut out to be here.* There was an outdoor space at the venue and since it was summertime it was still light outside even though it was the evening. I stayed outside after everyone had gone in to watch the band. I thought I was alone in this little courtyard and was about to start crying when I realized a friend I knew from college was out there too. We waved at each other and made our way across the courtyard to talk. We were having a polite convo about this and that, and after a few minutes of what-have-you-been-up-to back-and-forth he finally blurts out, "My dad just died."

I look back at him like *WTF, are you making fun of me?* and say, "What? My dad just died too." And now it's his turn to look at me like *WTF* and reply, "That's not funny." And I'm like "No, I'm serious. My dad died a few weeks ago," to which he replies, "Mine too." At that point, there is nothing left to do but cry. We both start crying. We don't know each other that well, but he'd always been a nice person and we can't stop crying. And now we are hugging and crying and, all of a sudden, this sadness feels more real than ever and also something that I can handle because I know someone else is going through the exact same thing.

We let go and pull ourselves together. We never speak of it again.

Olivia Lineberry

(zookeeper)

As I write this, I'm told of the passing of another animal. I've been a zookeeper for four years now and have worked with a huge variety of taxa. I have come to know well over one hundred individuals over the years. I spend just as much time at work with these guys as I do with my own at home. So, when it's time to say goodbye, it hurts just the same.

My team are all respectful of how each person grieves. We even have designated places that we have deemed best for crying: inside the zoo van, behind the goat barn, in the tortoise yard.

A brown-and-white guinea pig, Luna, who looked like a little baked potato, far surpassed her life expectancy but didn't wake up from anesthesia. We weren't prepared, so we didn't say goodbye beforehand. I wasn't at work when it happened, so I cried at home when I was told the news.

An owl, part of a species notorious for hiding any medical issues until it's too late, suddenly passed. Her name was Sophie. Again, we

didn't get to say goodbye. I went and sat with the tortoises after her necropsy.

It's exhausting, to be honest, but the love I feel toward them outweighs it, and the grief becomes part of the job description. I hope that the life I gave them was good enough, that they were happy. All I can do is continue giving the others my time and love, while looking back on the photos I have of them.

Chad Luibl

(literary agent)

When I was in third grade my mom bought me a copy of *Flowers for Algernon* by Daniel Keyes. I had just graduated from the Boxcar Children and she must've figured I was mature enough to handle it because all she said was "You're going to read this next and it'll make you cry." On the cover was a young couple dressed in corduroys and autumn sweaters, leaning over a lake and trying to scoop leaves out of the water. The book looked too adult, and therefore boring, and I couldn't understand her logic of measuring a book's value in tears.

Obviously, my mom knew I was a lonely and difficult kid, desperate for attention. It was the same summer that I volunteered to be an altar boy at our church—when I pretended the altar was a stage, and the churchgoers my friends, but at home, alone in my room, I drank stolen holy water, hoping it would wash away whatever angst I was already feeling at nine years old. My mom handed me that book and I was confused—I didn't want to cry, I wanted to feel joy.

I stormed up to my room.

I read it in one day and bawled my eyes out.

Over the years I've cried to many novels. Mary Shelley's *Frankenstein* got me a couple times in high school. Raymond Carver nearly killed me in undergrad. And nearly thirty years after *Flowers*, I've used it as a gauge to measure many of the books I've worked on in my publishing career. Did it make me cry? Is it that good?

Now I have a four-year-old daughter, and I'm the one gifting books. We read two or three stories every night before bedtime under the soft glow of a ladybug lamp, her sound machine gently whirring under the window. Last week, it was another childhood favorite, *The Giving Tree* by Shel Silverstein. The last page shows an elderly man sitting on his beloved tree stump—his most loyal friend—as he contemplates all of life's fleeting gifts, made precious by their transience. We lingered on that image, that final line— "And the tree was happy"—her hair still wet from the bath and drying on my shoulder.

Dr. Enongo Lumumba-Kasongo

(rapper, beatmaker, Pisces, performs as Sammus)

For me, crying is freedom. I've always found it easy to cry, although for most of my life I also felt great shame about being such a crybaby, even among close friends. When I first began writing and performing rap songs under the moniker Sammus in 2010, I approached my new persona primarily as a space to exhibit a cooler version of myself. But, with each song, she slowly transformed into a vessel for me to let the not-so-cool parts of my being run wild and free. By the time I landed my first tour in March of 2015 I found myself fighting back tears and often breaking down entirely on the stage every time I performed my freshly written track "1080p." Then just one verse, it was about my struggles as a Black woman navigating a PhD program while managing a chronic illness and trying to reconcile the abrupt end of a toxic love story. I recall the heat in my cheeks, and the discomfort on people's faces, the first time I sobbed in the middle of the song. I also recall the people who thanked me, hugged me, and cried with me at the merch table afterward. But even more than that, I remember the full-bodied tears that flowed the final time that I performed "1080p" on that tour, sixteen hundred miles from home on a stage in Austin at my first

SXSW and feeling gratitude for the reminder that a world existed beyond the cloud cover of my couch.

As soon as I got home, I wrote the second verse of the song:

Been a few months since the last verse
Since I called you bad words
I went ahead and got my masters
I trimmed the last of my relaxer
So my 'fro big
Got some mo' gigs
My cell phone says I'm roaming
Cuz I'm on tour
I want more
Forget home, so I go big
I was taking pills up in the bathroom
—ended up alone in grad school
I'm Mario I busted ass but
My prize is sitting in another castle
In a tight spot trying to disappear
I would write songs for my friends to hear
—I'm tryna keep my lights on
I'm a Nikon now it's crystal clear
Opportunity is at my doorstep
So I'm moving back up on the horse like
It's the first time I ever wore specks
Now I do my thing like life's a Rorschach
I see things nobody sees
Since my bee stings turned to double ds
I'm conceding
That my feelings
Is amazing

Now I'm lovin' me!
I could give it up but where's the fun in that?
Gotta live it up or you will never laugh
Life's a box of chocolates with a lot of options
Gotta keep it rocking life's a rumble pack
The first letter of your first name
Makes your name emerge when I search things
And it hurts me but I guarantee
That without you I'm a better me
Now I see the past with some clarity
Glad I took my ass to some therapy
Now I'm seeing the world in 1080p
Now I'm seeing my world in 1080p

Kathy Macleod

(cartoonist, author of Continental Drifter*)*

Last week
I couldn't
stop crying

I cried as soon
as I woke up

I cried while
meditating

I cried in
the shower

I cried on
the train

I cried alone

I cried with
friends

I cried listening
to music

and in the silence
before falling asleep

And it didn't feel like depression

Depression
(for me)

Whatever the hell was going on last week

To be fair, there is a lot to cry about right now. The world feels like it's falling apart even though my life is objectively okay even though the world feels like it's falling apart even though...

The view from the Internet

The view from my window

When I cry or feel sad
it is always exacerbated
by these other internal
factors:

Why are you sad What's
wrong with you Things
are going well in your
life Are you stupid

→ relentless
self-bullying

STOP CRYING
YOU ARE BAD FOR
CRYING STOP BEING
WEAK GO TO YOUR ROOM

childhood
stuff

I try to combat
them with various
meditation techniques/
radical self-acceptance
and so on.

you're going
through major
life changes

of course
you'll feel
up and down

It's okay—
this belongs

it's all
part of
the same
ocean

you are
not this
feeling

you are
the ocean

I learned a German saying for someone who cries easily – "Nah am Wasser gebaut"

"Built too close to the water"

I like the sound of that. Because crying feels like a conduit for something natural and pure.

That is, when you're not fighting against it, when you're just letting the current flow by.

Maral

(producer, DJ, label A&R, helper of
growing a healthy music ecosystem)

On June 9, 2022, the musician Julee Cruise passed away from suicide at the age of sixty-five. She suffered from horrible health issues and in the words of her husband, "She left this realm on her own terms. No regrets. She is at peace."

I had spent many years crying to her music, sometimes because of sorrow in my own life, but most of the time from the sheer beauty and pureness of her music. I spent the whole day in tears when I learned of her death, thinking about her journey, her legacy, and the impact it's had on me and so many others. I cried thinking about how our health has an impact on our ability to enjoy the world—and continue adding value to it. This coincided with feelings of sadness and dread I have in relation to my own physical health and how its limitations are a constant source of frustration and tears. But Julee's story showed me that even within those limitations you can have a profound impact and create a legacy, that there is beauty in between the tears.

I have those moments of reflection and tears often with music, especially from the music of women who have struggled and who had their time cut short. (Like, for instance, the legendary Iranian singer Hayedeh, who represents so much to the Iranian people. Every time I listen to her songs, I—and, I think, every Iranian—shed a communal tear.)

There is a longing in these women's music, for something beyond their reach and beyond the reach of almost every woman in the music industry. They've had to withstand so much just to get the chance to share their art with the world. I cry thinking about their struggles. I also shed tears of joy that we have the gift of their music.

Most of my tears nowadays stem from my frustrations with the music industry and the slow disintegration of any sort of support system for artists outside of the mainstream. This is a constant topic in my therapy sessions. This feeling of helplessness luckily diminishes whenever I'm in community spaces and supportive underground zones. The exchange of appreciation and support within a community helps you feel like even though you might be hindered in some ways due to isolating health issues, that what you *are* doing is impactful and is helping to fertilize the ecosystem. Good music can be transcendent. It helps reset me. That's the thing: in between the tears, I'm still a member of the music ecosystem.

Sammy Maine

(writer, reader, manager, tour manager)

When I had finally mustered up the courage to visit my mum in rehab, the first thing I noticed was the fluorescent lighting. It gave the bags under her eyes a buzzing spotlight, forcing me to reckon with a face that had been hiding itself for most of my childhood. My big brother, unsure of what to do with his limbs, stood with his hands in his pockets, while our father filled out paperwork at the front desk. We made small talk with a person we didn't recognize:

—How's the food?

—Have you made any friends?

It was the same conversation we'd had for years, as my brother and I regularly navigated new classrooms, new accents, new rules. Our mum remained as mute as we had.

As a military family, we were used to upheaval. And yet, despite our shared, shaky foundation, my brother and I had been careful not to hold on to each other. Perhaps my brother, swimming in the same nervousness, felt the need to portray a sort of big brother caricature: one who made fun of me for watching *Power Rangers*, punched my arms, and placed giant dill pickles in my mouth as I slept. That way, we always knew our place, no matter the location.

Since the night our home was drenched in red and blue lights, I had remained numb. Friends probed at my stoicism as we walked to school. My father tried to get me to eat. But the bleach that filled my nose in that foreign living room triggered a kind of crumbling: one I wasn't ready for. I inhaled it, hoping it would rid my body of the color of catastrophe. My brother, maybe noticing the flicker in my eyes, gestured us over to the guest book. There, in his typically boyish ledger, it read: *I SEE DEAD PEOPLE.* He smirked, and in a baby sister mimic, I smirked too. We could no longer contain it: this absurdity, the challenge of it, 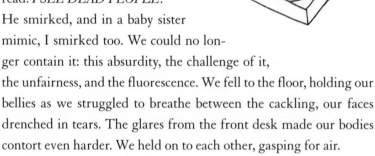 the unfairness, and the fluorescence. We fell to the floor, holding our bellies as we struggled to breathe between the cackling, our faces drenched in tears. The glares from the front desk made our bodies contort even harder. We held on to each other, gasping for air.

In the car, our father asked us what we wanted for dinner. In unison, my brother and I declared, "Pizza." Our eyes—still damp—met in the rearview mirror.

Aanchal Malhotra

(oral historian, novelist)

Seated in a sunlit living room in Lahore in 2014, I had asked my interviewee about his migration during the 1947 Partition of British India as a part of the field research for a book project. His family had left their home in Jullundur, India, fleeing violence, and traveled for days from camp to camp, often in the hours ungoverned by curfew, until they finally reached Pakistan. "How did you feel? Were you not afraid? You were only a teenager, after all." I looked up from my notebook to find his gentle face turned toward the window, looking beyond the landscape outside, perhaps even—I had thought at the time—into the past.

It was then that it happened. So far, I had been privy to visceral, aged sorrow, to confusion, anger, loss, pain, silence, and even helplessness, but never tears. Despite these conversations penetrating, at times, the most traumatic moments of people's lives, no one had cried in my presence. But tears laced the gentleman's eyes and began trickling down his long face. He was eighty-three years old, exactly six decades my senior, and in my attempt to cross the boundaries of our nationalities, religions, and generations, I felt I'd arrived at the threshold of my questioning. I was motionless, struck by the reversal of our roles: the old and the young, my memories immediately scurried across the border to my grandmother in Delhi, remembering how she wiped my eyes dry when I cried as a child.

The gentleman continued to look out the window and I continued to look at him, as the recorder continued to record the gentle sounds of breathing and crying, against the background of the whirring ceiling fan. Then, he brought his hands to his eyes, massaging them through the tears, and asked me in Urdu, "Aap agar ek paudhe ko apni zameen se nikaal kar kisi aur zameen mein daalenge, toh panapne mein samay toh lagega na? Aur phir shayad woh ugay hi na." *If you uproot a sapling from its natural habitat and try to transplant it elsewhere, the chances of it growing and thriving are slim—and perhaps it may not live at all. This is how it had felt."*

Things born from a certain land belonged to that land alone, I remember transcribing in my notebook.

Jilian Medford

*(musician, performs as Ian Sweet,
Coldplay's biggest fan, Blueberry's mom)*

'm obsessed with crying. It's really one of my favorite things to do. I think that anyone who listens to my music can immediately tell I'm a big crier. Practically every other song references bawling my eyes out. Crying makes me feel powerful and released from the grasp of my always-spinning mind. It gives me the opportunity to give in and surrender to something bigger than myself and let go of control, if even for a moment. Whenever I do one of those really big, weepy, healing, snot-dripping-into-my-mouth-and-down-my-chin kind of cries, it feels like I've just watered all the plants in my mind, put them out in the sun, and watched them grow and bloom a little bit more. It's a never-ending process of having to water yourself: empty the bucket and let it fill up again.

I have been feeling my most vulnerable and emotional while out on the road post-COVID. For the last two years I could cry alone in my house, freely and as much and as loudly as I'd liked. Being on tour, surrounded by people constantly and being the leader of the band, I find myself holding back tears, because I don't want to affect anyone else's experience. But the moments where I'm pretending

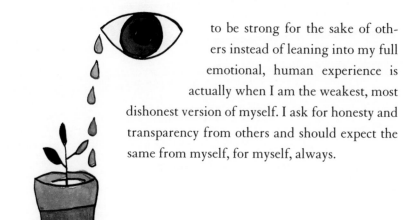

to be strong for the sake of others instead of leaning into my full emotional, human experience is actually when I am the weakest, most dishonest version of myself. I ask for honesty and transparency from others and should expect the same from myself, for myself, always.

Caits Meissner

*(writer, poet, comic artist, curator, director of Prison
and Justice Writing at PEN America)*

S top smiling!"
    The room admonishes me in unison, with light in their
voices. I have been tapped to play Evillene in an amateur production of *The Wiz*. So, I stand in a classroom before a half circle of
women in prison greens, proving my discomfort with an apologetic
grin rather than the shadowy grimace of the wicked.

How did I end up here?

My audition was simple: I was to repeat the three octaves sung
by a music instructor in the prison's hallway, and *boom!*, the gig I
didn't know I was applying for was mine. Now I am the only civil-
ian woman in the play, a last-minute call-in when an incarcerated
actor was abruptly transferred to a facility farther upstate.

My qualifications include a well-worn clearance that allows me
entrance, a passable singing voice, and six days of availability the
week before the show. I have an additional week to learn my lines
and all of the songs, which I will now use part of a long-planned
writing residency to conquer.

I am wildly uncomfortable with all of it, and so I say yes.

• • •

The actors have already been at it a year and change, and I am, quite clearly, the bumbling novice. A blush climbs me like a vine when I sing "No Bad News." I project with my poet voice while delivering my lines, but the effect is stunted and cheesy.

When water is thrown in my direction (pantomimed from an empty bucket), I pull the blue satin cape over my head as if melting, squealing the wicked witch's famous phrase as I scurry backward off the stage. This move is perhaps the most embarrassing. The crouching feels animalistic. My voice, as I pretend to diminish into air, is cartoonish and unbelievable.

But moreover, what stays with me long after the stage is the recognition that the act feels weighted with metaphor.

The actors are mostly students of mine who have revealed themselves, sometimes slowly, sometimes with urgency, over the past three years in a weekly intensive poetry seminar. In the prison classroom where we meet for three hours a session, the ritualized roll of toilet paper is always kicked from the center of our circle into someone's hands and lands in another's.

In our room, the women come to share the intricacies of their emotional lives more than to study the craft of writing. The generative process is a vehicle for expression, so desperately needed that what is revealed can often be downright shocking in its pain—experienced and perpetrated alike.

I am melting.

Some stories are unbearable, some even unbelievable—and, indeed, they might be. We're after emotional truth, not necessarily the facts. Like fiction, a good fib in the form of a story can just as easily crack the heart's fruit and allow for a profound, physical release. In a landscape where sharing your scars is often weaponized, the relief in being able to cry is palpable. Whatever brings it to the surface, in my opinion, is welcome.

In contrast, I never cry in my witnessing, even when it means blinking back tears. It is my role to hold the space and I take the charge seriously. Though sometimes I do allow the water to pour from me on the train ride home, creating a private curtain of self-produced rain. I look out the dark window as the sleepy upstate towns pass with their quaint lights, so far from the cages my students lock themselves into at night.

Preparations for the play happen in a room across the hall, a different room from our lessons. Today, I am the student being coached toward more villainy by incarcerated women. This is a fact we laugh about, given its implications, what it points to. It is the kind of laughter that can only be shared with trust—out of someone else's mouth, *don't even*. One of the most surprising facts to the prison-curious is that there is abundant laughter: jokes and comedian-level self-deprecation abound. Of course, what makes the joke funny—this cheeky invitation to step deeper into my villainous role, a label applied to my costars, so says the state—is its tether to reality, how the power dynamics are so crudely baked into our respective roles. I am well-attuned to the fact that I come and go from the prison in my own clothing. I am not subjected to routine pat-downs by guards. I sleep in my own bed at night.

Still, for six days I fold myself into the collective in a manner I'd never be allowed as facilitator. I eat the brown bag lunch with its slimy ham sandwich alongside the women in their state-issued greens. I prop myself on the gymnasium tables and copy dance moves out of the corner of my eye onstage.

It is the most unrestricted I've been able to move among these women I've known for years now—many through stories of profoundly intimate, violent, painful secrets—and in between rehearsing I catch all sorts of new gossip: who is struggling with the dance moves, who is in love with who, whose sentences are extended or up for commutation, who has had a recent visit, who is fighting whom, and, most excitingly, how one makes a strap-on in prison (with a plastic toothbrush container, jelly, surgical gloves, and an Ace bandage).

There is a marked difference between the rooms we occupy— the poetry room, the theater room. Here, the charge is collaboration, the teamwork necessary to pull off a show. That doesn't mean we forgo tension, of course, but I take note of how, throughout the week, all eyes remain on the prize. There's not a tear in sight.

During our final rehearsal I become acquainted with my dance partner: a life-size plastic skeleton.

Aside from this being another reason to feel embarrassed about my own lack of grace, I have no feelings one way or another about the symbol. It's a Halloween store purchase, a science class prop, a decidedly neutral object in the schema of my existence.

"Probably better you than her to be dancing with that thing," someone says, nodding to the woman originally meant to play Evillene, who is now cast in the lead role, in part thanks to her photographic memory.

"Can you imagine this prisoner dancing with a skeleton onstage when she's denied killing her husband in a conspiracy all those years ago?"

The media coverage of her case was unprecedented—and the press whipped up a storm of drama, accusing her of a cold heart, of being distant in the courtroom, her stoic gaze seeking some distant horizon, no tears at all. Ice queen. Bitch. Evil witch?

Though I found this woman to be brilliant—a poem about never having children seared itself into my heart one semester—and undeniably respected and dedicated to helping others, I have to admit that when I watched the coverage, I also felt a pang of questioning. The lack of tears seemed suspect. The narrative I've inherited is that women cry. A lot. It's how we know we are alive.

What are we to deduce when a woman does not cry? Does this make her less believable? Less sympathetic to the possibility that she was a victim too? Less worthy of redemption, even if the case was sealed in hard facts, and therefore she's never, ever, no matter what, able to live outside these prison walls? Never even able to petition for the possibility?

When the day arrives, the gym is a flutter of nerves. We are preparing for two performances. The first, in the morning, will find us singing to an audience of all incarcerated women, and the second, at night, the room will fill with friends and family—a first for the prison.

Nikki, who was born in the same hospital as me—a fact that once cracked her airtight facade as a newbie in our emotionally charged class—now braids my hair in a loose French-style. Her fingers, once known for this skill during her previous life as a hairstylist, are the sweet fingers of a little sister on my scalp.

We are in the makeshift greenroom, the locker room of the gymnasium, and I keep one eye on the guard. I don't want to be ejected from the prison on the grounds of overfriendliness. A simple hug is enough to get one's program canceled.

Nikki was never one to cry, her mean mug so perfected that

winning a one-sided smile was a victory. A few words on the page, a feat.

As the comb tenderly brushes my scalp, I can feel the sacred exchange in this act. Nikki nuzzles up to me, through this task disguised as necessary for the show. It is emotional, though it is quiet.

Now I understand that Nikki cries through her fingers.

The play was chosen by the women because of its connection to the experience of incarceration. I have, of course, understood the profundity of the musical's songs in this context, but I don't feel them in my body until I am standing in a line onstage next to women transformed by their costumes, lifted momentarily out of prison and into another scene. Together, in a dizzyingly honest array of wonderful and off-key voices, we sing—

When I think of home
I think of a place where there's love overflowing

In the morning, I look into the audience and see a sea of women in green. I see the crossed arms and slow gum chew of the hardened, those determined not to be made soft, but I am practiced at sensing a glimmer of curiosity, even joy, under the facade. I see faces awash in the waterfall of tears. At night, I see the faces of my students' loved ones. In both audiences, more are crying than not. I lift my hand to my cheeks and discover—so am I.

In a short documentary following the performance day, the star of the short film is Dunasha, who played Glinda the Good Witch in our production. She is smiling when she confesses her crime to the camera—pumped up on the adrenaline of performance, her big grin is incongruent with the words coming out of her mouth. I am angered by this cheap directive from the filmmakers, how insensitive, what the moment seems to imply.

I know Dunasha well, and have many times seen tears make their paths on her cheeks. She is open and searching, formerly a pre-med student, now questioning how to parent through the walls. In the video she shares her homecoming plan, two years in the future. Dunasha will package herself in a large box, gift-wrap it, and jump out to her daughter's delight: Surprise! Dunasha will be home two days before Christmas. The other story that seeded itself into my memory was shared in our poetry room: Dunasha told her daughter the hand and feet cuffs were bracelets when on temporary furlough for a family funeral.

Dunasha has always been generous with her tears. In the documentary Dunasha is crying too.

She says to the camera, "I made a mistake and it's a chance for me to do better. I'm young, I'm twenty-four years old . . . Just because I made a mistake it doesn't mean that my heart is not good . . . This gives me the chance to show that I am somebody, that I am loving, that I do cry."

The camera pans to the audience, where her daughter, age five, sits on a family member's lap, watching her mother, not in the visiting room in prison greens, but onstage in a glittering cape and pillbox hat. Dunasha is reaching up toward the sky with her church-honed voice. She is singing, "Believe in yourself." She is singing to her daughter.

Her eyes are dry. They are shining.

Eileen Myles

(poet, author of a "Working Life")

Our fights were clean because I'd stroll off and have a drink somewhere alone and I liked that. I was sort of looking for my father in bars. He'd been dead for eighteen years by then, but bars were where I found him. But this was in the afternoon, so instead I went to the mall. The mall in Boulder in 1979 was this strange combination of postmodern and hippy, the way Boulder was then. The money had started to come in, so there were new details like the mall itself and the frog fountain and the deliberate gathering places where Peter was singing. I saw the crowd without knowing what was inside it. It was Peter Orlovsky being a fool and he was such a handsome one. He had a guitar and was singing songs in that deliberately dumb way he had that seemed like a person from the lower classes doing that, but in a different mode. Plus, he was singing about his butthole, which no one working-class would ever do except that Peter had been bred by the Beats. I stood there watching, then I shoved to the front of the crowd 'cause I had been trained that way at rock concerts, the front counts, and then it started to happen. I was thinking about Allen and Peter and their great love. I was thinking about me and her and how fucked it was, and how I loved being inside the world with someone and here I was outside with no one, and I started to cry. It was sort of comforting to cry in a crowd surrounded by all these strange people looking at something else. I was safe to weep my ass off, really sobbing. Peter's butthole joy was 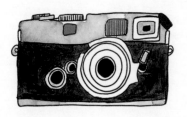 my heaving-lonely-eyeholes-poet me from Boston, twenty-nine years old here because I was beginning to be a famous poet too, but I was no one now, had nothing, had no one—and then I saw the camera. It was Nam June Paik whirling his camera around, shooting everyone. It has happened to me once or twice in the past, feeling really exposed already but in a secret way and then strangely caught in a lens. It felt profound, I felt like Buddha. Here I was; get my face. And when I walked into the Whitney ten years later and he had all those TVs stacked one on top of the other, and in one quick moment there was my sobbing face. I was young, it was beautiful, it was wonderful. Can I have that footage now? I want it back.

Elle Nash

(writer, author of Deliver Me*)*

You left me during the longest days of the year. You left me with all the administration it takes to raise a family, build a home— you left it all to me. You left because your home is on fire and the old country couldn't keep you.

I didn't cry then, not yet.

I burrowed into family graves, rubbing my fingers into the granite voids: 1642, 1623, how far back that woman was buried into the floor of the crumbling church. Sweeping green lawn, untended, like a meadow. The sweet smell of worms and wet mulch. Grass crawling out from the brick retaining walls like spider legs.

Every day I wake up and draw a circle. Not being able to kiss or touch is its own kind of hell. A thousand desires couldn't run me this ragged.

Body builds an organ. Body builds a home. Nobody comes. Body destroys the home. Moon pulls at the insides, red tide, blank hooks, barnacles on rocks. Body becomes barren. Body doesn't fuck. Body builds a temple. Loneliness is a god. Placenta-dark, a thing burrows in. All the moss-wet rock inside, somewhere there is life amoebic. I curve fetal into my old mother, my mother which is loneliness. I love how dark she is. The way her smell wraps around me like a shawl. Her love is abandonment. Abandonment is how she loves. I let go, finally, but am I crying for you? The answer is far, waiting in the rain, in the beautiful, beautiful hills. And there you are rising from the mist, leaving this terrible wake behind you.

Nora Neus

(journalist)

People are always apologizing to me for crying. Even though their seventeen-year-old son was just gunned down in his classroom by a shooter with an AR-15. Even though their home was just swept away by an EF4 tornado, leaving nothing but cotton-candy-colored insulation drifting on their lawn. Even though they were just buried alive by a Russian air strike, dust coating the inside of their pink throats, and only barely survived to tell their story.

"Sorry," they say, "I'll get it together."

As if they have something to be embarrassed about.

"Please, don't worry," I say. "It's understandable that you're crying," I say. "I'm going to break down in tears as soon as I get home anyway," I don't say.

There are unwritten rules in journalism about whose tears are allowed.

The grieving mother? Yes.

The traumatized survivor? Yes.

The reporter listening to their stories, sinuses itchy with unshed tears? No.

Much of that has good reasons: The focus should be on the

subject, not the journalist. Reporters shouldn't make it about us. We have a job to do, one that deserves our full focus.

There's also this sense that they're not my tears to cry. *My* child wasn't just murdered in a nation where we do nothing to prevent school shootings from happening. *My* cozy apartment in Brooklyn is waiting for me a short flight away, where *my* partner is likely doing laundry so I come home to warm, clean sheets on the bed.

And yet.

The metallic taste is at my tongue. And sometimes, for all the biting the insides of my cheeks I can do, the tears spill over.

And sometimes, I think that's OK.

Why shouldn't we cry hot tears at the injustices we see and the traumas to which we bear witness? Why shouldn't we show that we too bleed, that we care? We are not neutral observers; we never could be. We bring our own life experiences with us to each story we report. And then we take each story we report back into our lives, carrying them with us like marbles in a box.

Most times, my own tears are shed in private, in a stuffy rental car that I parked too long in direct sunlight, or in a Marriott hotel room so blandly decorated that I wake up and forget, for just a moment, what city I'm in. Most times, my own tears are shed after the day's work is done.

These tears are important. They remind me I'm human. And they bring me back to the moment, four gas-station coffees and two suitcase granola bars ago, when someone else was wiping away their tears as they trusted me with their story, their truth, and their most fragile memories.

Zannie Owens

(musician, poet, gardener, puppeteer, performs as Zannie)

For all at last return to the sea—to Oceanus, the ocean river, like the ever-flowing stream of time, the beginning and the end.

—Rachel Carson, *The Sea Around Us*

What crabs? Are you mad? What crabs? Ah! Yes. Well, yes . . . The crabs are men. And so? Where did I get that idea? Real men, good and beautiful, on all the balconies of the centuries. As for me, I was crawling in the yard; I imagined I heard them speaking: "Brother, what's that?" That was me. Me the Crab . . . Well, I said no: my age will not be judged by men. What will such men be, after all? The sons of our sons. Can one permit brats to condemn their grandfathers? I turned the situation round; I yelled: 'Here is man; apres moi, le déluge; apres le déluge, crabs, you!' Unmasked, all of them! The balconies were swarming with arthropods.

—Jean-Paul Sartre, *The Condemned of Altona*

1. Emotional crying is a uniquely human experience.
2. Animals keep evolving into crabs.

et us attempt to force these ideas together! Much in the way evolution tried to force the blueprint of crab upon other oceanic entities throughout time. "Carcinization" is the term for the repetitive convergent (will the tears also?) evolution from non-crab crustaceans into crab forms. This process transpired on at least five separate occasions that we're aware of. It's been suggested there could be an evolutionary advantage to crab form,

To scuttle between land and sea, Temperance . . .

otherwise, this phenomenon has yet to be explained.

Kankros, the Proto-Italic ancestor of *cancer* (the Latin term for crab), comes from the word *karkros*, meaning enclosure. This was attributed to the crab's pincers forming a circle when closed.

Is fate a circle?
The enclosure of the earth's biosphere
The enclosure of water that is the ocean
The steady enclosure of crab

The Greek cognate of *cancer* is "karkínos":

καρκῖνος • (karkínos) m (genitive καρκῖνου); second declension

1. crab
2. Cancer, the zodiac sign

3. sore, ulcer, cancer
4. items which resemble a crab's pincers [some of which have been redacted for the sake of concision]:
   a. pair of pincers, a type of torture instrument
   b. temple bones
   c. pair of compasses
   d. distillery

In pop astrology, the sign Cancer is often associated with tears. This sign is ruled by the moon, which controls the ocean's tides, crab molting cycles, and perhaps also our moods. The glyph for Cancer is a sideways 69, designed to represent the crab's claws or a mother's breast (in honor of the nurturing nature of this archetype).

To pinch then pull the thread dangling from the hem of woven crab mythos adorning the primordial Mother Crab herself

Crabs don't cry.

But do they feel pain? Yes! Let's dispel the myth they don't. A myth almost as cruel as Hercules kicking the giant crab Karkinos so far into the heavens it became the constellation Cancer.

Using the cloth to dry our tears . . .

1. The eyelids pince together to release tears.
2. The temples ache after a long cry.
3. Human eyes contain the protein cryptochrome, an organic compass that senses the Earth's magnetic field.
4. These eyes are, of course, also responsible for the distillation of tears.

Our primate ancestors' eyes evolved to be forward-facing so they could easily grasp fruit from trees. Perhaps the forbidden fruit in the book of Genesis was a crab apple.

Crabs have the opposite layering of a human being. Bone on the outside, muscle inside.

Casting a wide net, but only pulling up salty mucous water

Crying is externalizing salty mucous water, much like submerging one's face in the ocean. The ocean has its own mucous: "marine mucilage," also known as sea snot.

One hypothesis as to why we cry (in addition to the soothing release of endorphins and oxytocin, which the crabs do also have!) is to signal emotion to others so they may offer support. Collectivizing joy and suffering, ideally allowing us to languish in that vast ocean of empathy—perhaps enclosed by one giant crab claw, free floating for ages in salty water and sea snot until what makes us so very human causes us to carcinize and we scuttle back to the shore again.

Taylor Palmby

(therapist, fitness instructor, lover of all things punk rock)

Music. Music always plays in the background as I accomplish my work as the tear keeper.

Sometimes the music is the soft jazz that comes from the lobby of my therapy office as my patients cry. Other times the music is the pounding EDM that fills my spin class. The intensity of sensation—pitch-black room, spirited beat drops, and pounding hearts—creates an environment where a motivational phrase can spark quiet tears to fall through the final push of a forty-five-minute class. My favorite tear-streaked moments consist somewhere between the two.

Like when sweaty, tired bodies file past me on their way between music stages. I give them a high five and ask them who they are here to see. I say something rushed about how my nonprofit supports those who are struggling with mental health. Moments later, a tent at Warped Tour transforms into a therapy office, the lack of ethical guidelines allowing me to hug this concertgoer as their tears stain my T-shirt.

Everywhere I go tears follow me, and music lulls me from moment to moment. Many have an aversion to this amount of emotional expression. They see it as exhausting, scary, and heartbreaking. I've come to see it as the opposite. In every space, I find tears to be heart-mending. The tears in a therapy office mean a patient has touched a part of them that needs to be seen, reflected, and empathized with. Once that happens, the tears don't stop—they fall harder. In a spin class, when the tears come it's almost always a client who "didn't want to come to class today" but showed up anyway, and the pride, community, and strength they experience help them build confidence that they can show up even when it's hard. The tears on tour often fall from the eyes of those who have been dying for anyone to ask them how they're feeling, and the sweet relief of moving out of their rock bottom and into their rising.

I keep the thousands of tears I've witnessed in my heart and carry them with me as I open my hands to hold the cries of the next human who sheds them on their journey through renewal.

Carissa Potter

(artist, author)

For my father's seventieth birthday, I got us tandem paragliding flights. This was not something I would ever do on my own.

Since moving to the bay in 2021 to help us during the pandemic, he has longed to hang-glide. Making trips to Fort Funston to gaze longingly at the humans soaring through the air. He wanted to be a pilot. He wants to be a bird. He has dreams he can fly. No one offers tandem hang-gliding flights anymore, or that I could find, so I went with paragliding. (To his disappointment, but whatever.)

We drove from Oakland to Pacifica, a city along the coast of California, and walked halfway up the seaside cliff, the ice plants in full bloom, sun shining. Waves rolling. I met my guide. His name was David. He was learning English. He was young. Without much warning, we strapped ourselves together and ran off the side of a cliff. Apparently, my father made a comment after we left about how there should have been more checking of the "rigs."

I don't know if it was the height, or the beauty of it all, or the cold, or whatever, but I cried. Not sobbing cry. But a silent cry. Strapped to this attractive stranger. I tried to make small talk. The only thing that came to mind was asking him if anyone had ever

vomited on him in the air? But I resisted as I felt my stomach churn. I didn't want to know. And I am trying to learn how to NOT ask questions when I know I will not like the answers.

We were both facing outward. So we couldn't look at each other. Which was for the best. I imagined what it would feel like to fall. To have our bodies embrace the sea. Or the side of the mountain. What a privilege to feel safe and terrified at the same time. There was a part of me, a small part of me, that felt okay if this was the end. And I thought about how if this was to be the end, I was somehow grateful to be with this stranger. Out of all the strangers. Grateful that our fates were intertwined.

"David, do people ever confess things to you while you are in the air?" He returned with, "What? I don't understand." I dropped it. And just cried while trying not to look down. I thought for a moment about telling him why I was crying. But decided that maybe it was best if he just assumed that it was from the altitude or something.

Sara Quin

(writer, musician, one half of Tegan and Sara)

The earliest days of the pandemic were rain-soaked and black. From my studio window in North Vancouver, I watched crows dive-bomb the black-capped chickadees that were perched on the bird feeders I'd hung in the cedar trees. Tour was canceled, and the fertility treatment my partner and I started a year earlier was suspended. It seemed that not only our lives were in limbo, but even the *possibility* of life. Fiddleheads poked out of the ferns in April, and I bought trays of hostas to plant next to them in the garden. Mom visited, at a distance, and together we dug holes in the damp soil. I took afternoon walks in Mosquito Creek, listening to audiobooks about murder and cancer. The dread and grief that had enveloped me during the early months of lockdown dissipated, and this new routine became comforting. There was another winter, a spring, and the hottest summer in a hundred years. Tegan got a pandemic puppy, we all got vaccines, and the familiar feeling of life, picking up speed, returned. In September we flew south, and recorded an album of songs about change, and *never* changing, and the nostalgia aching in both our bones. As we started our final week in the studio, my partner sent me a photograph of a positive pregnancy test. Cry, baby.

T. Cole Rachel

(writer, poet, editor, ceramic cat enthusiast)

On April 11, 2019, I was at the Will Rogers World Airport in Oklahoma City, on my way back to New York City after visiting my dad, who was in the middle of being treated for stage 4 throat cancer. After totally white-knuckling it through a day of goodbyes with my various family members, I managed to hold off on having a meltdown until making it through security and finding my gate. Confronted with the idea that—depending on what may or may not happen—it was possible that I might not ever see my dad again, the floodgates finally opened. The funny thing about it was that I was also starving and had impulse-purchased a box of mini Cinnabons on my way in. So I spent an hour at my gate openly bawling and cramming tiny cinnamon rolls into my face. Later, after landing in New York, I went to the bathroom at JFK and realized that I'd traveled all the way home with white cinnamon glaze all over one side of my face. I started crying again.

Austin Louis Ray

(writer, dad, creator of How I'd Fix Atlanta*)*

The first time Jens Lekman made me cry was the summer of 2007. I was twenty-five years old, working for a music magazine. I happened upon an advance copy of his second album, *Night Falls Over Kortedala*, and was immediately taken with it. In the time since, I could easily call any number of the songs on that album My Favorite Jens Lekman Song, but at the time, the first one that really got me was "A Postcard to Nina."

It does more than any five minutes of pop music has a right to, frankly, detailing a charming encounter that takes place while Jens and his friend Nina are enjoying some time together in Berlin. Everything is going great until they walk up to Nina's dad's apartment for dinner and Nina informs Jens that he needs to pretend to be her boyfriend. You see, her dad wouldn't approve of the truth, which is that she's a lesbian, so Nina opts to give him some fiction instead. Jens is an unwilling participant, but it's too late.

The trio have their meal together, it's understandably awkward, and Jens tries to say the right things to Nina's dad to impress him. (Incidentally, it works a little too well and the dad emails Jens "all the time" following the meetup.)

It's funny in the way that having friends around family members can be funny, but also sad in ways that are obviously deeper. By the end, we learn that the song is actually a postcard from Jens. And then there's that moment that really got me, that always really gets me. He says he just wants to check in with her, that he's been thinking about their time with her father a lot, and that he just wanted to say "don't let anyone stand in your way."

There's a minute or so of the song left at this point, and Jens opts to spend that minute singing "DON'T LET ANYONE STAND IN YOUR WAY!" He doesn't scream it exactly, but he really lets it fly, he belts it, and it's just so triumphant and beautiful, its message so true and pure. It seems only fitting to type it in all caps. It's the culmination of a story that's full of cringe moments, embarrassing little relatable exchanges, and a much bigger issue bubbling just below the surface. It's the difficult and righteous answer that so many of us must accept, since we live in a world where so many others are going to stand in our way when we simply want to be ourselves. It's incredible.

(A quick parenthetical aside: a decade and a half after releasing *Kortedala*, Jens rereleased the album under a new name—*The Linden Trees Are Still in Blossom*—with new arrangements for the original songs plus a few completely new songs. It's an unusual move for an artist, one that apparently had something to do with the fact that when Jens released *Kortedala* he was still fairly under the radar as far as singer-songwriters go, and as such, perhaps didn't perform as much due diligence as he should've with respect to some samples on the album.

But anyway, he releases this new version of an old album, and it's predictably lovely. If you're a *Kortedala* superfan, you can sit there and listen to this new version of it loudly in your living room all afternoon, yelling out things like "That's a new drum fill!" and "He cut out the horns here!" until all your loved ones vacate the premises.

All the new arrangements and embellishments and omissions are delightful to behold. It's like meeting up with an old friend after many years and discovering the new elements of their personality that are scattered throughout a whole that still feels comfortable, relaxing, good. But it was the title song, "The Linden Trees Are Still in Blossom," that really stopped me in my tracks on that first listen.

The song is a follow-up to "A Postcard to Nina," in which Lekman tries to reconnect with her. He sings that a recent email to Nina bounced back and since she doesn't use social media, he's found himself anxiously filling in the blanks as to her whereabouts. While wondering if their friendship fizzled or if he could've been better at staying in touch, his memories wander back to high school, where he and Nina first became pen pals—he in Sweden, she in Germany. As he reminisces back to the present, he sings that his fans have asked about her over the years, that some of them wondered if she was real, but that others, in places where homosexuality is oppressed or punished, knew that she was real. They understood her pain.

Eventually, he notes that "Sometimes I think about your father, how he turned a 180 soon after. I hope you've been able to reconcile, it must be hard, but I know you'd try. If you see him, please say hi." This line fucking *levels* me every time I hear it, a reminder that things are getting better even when it seems like they're not, that people often grow and evolve

and change their ignorant opinions, that maybe we don't have to fear for our future.)

But back to 2007. I remember sitting there: hunched in my cubicle and trying to be cool and subtle about it, wearing my stupid little earbuds plugged into my crummy old laptop that the music magazine didn't even pay for, hiding there in the semi-dark silence of the office, listening to this affecting story with the life-affirming payoff, and crying. It felt *good*. It was the start of a lifelong appreciation of an artist's body of work, a reminder of what music could be and the feelings it could inspire. I no longer write about music for a living, but it was one of those moments that reminded me why I did, one that forever changed how I feel about art in general.

Over the years, I've cried countless times to this song and to plenty of his other songs, both live and on record. I've cried while sad, sometimes, sure. But other times while happy, intentionally putting on his music because I knew it would give me self-fulfilling tears. Sometimes the feeling sneaks up on you, other times you know it's coming.

The latest—and certainly not last—time Jens Lekman made me cry was the summer of 2022. I was thirty-nine years old, and I was sitting on my couch at 5:57 a.m. on a Wednesday, quietly listening to "A Postcard to Nina," hoping not to wake up my sleeping family while trying to find the right words for a book about crying. I marveled at how much had changed in the past fifteen years, finding some comfort in knowing that songs like this are always right there waiting for you if you need them. If you want, you can sit there and you can cry and it will feel great. And so that's what I did, while writing this essay for you.

claire rousay

(amateur)

it's 4 p.m. on a monday and i cannot stop sobbing.
i haven't been able to eat or sleep or leave the bed for days. crying
    every single day for the past twenty days.
now that i type it out, that seems like an obvious red flag . . .
    something is wrong.

on paper, my life is nice.
actually, my life is becoming the very life i have dreamed about
    since i was a little kid.
i so badly wish i could engage, appreciate, and truly LIVE this life
    that i've been fortunate enough to experience. unfortunately,
    there is a seemingly infinite void inside of me.
and a darkness that won't lift.

i have never felt this alone and discarded in my life.
this includes times when i lost friends, family, and even what i
    thought was my god.

perhaps those losses just compounded, including my current
     situational stressors (?).
or maybe this is unrelated. or maybe i am making it all up.

i am writing this on my iPhone,
and can already tell that this text will
     either end up sounding like
     a suicide note or, like, some
     pathetic attempt at "being
     real."

it is neither though. the
     closest thing i can think
     of to compare this text to
     is a letter to the universe,
     begging for the aching to let
     up, the crying to slow, and my
     ability to function to return.

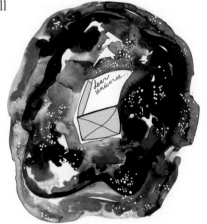

sometimes i am just grateful that i can still cry—because being
     numb is an even worse reality, and very few people seem to
     return from that.

Liara Roux

(sex worker, organizer, author of Whore of New York*)*

I love crying. All my friends have seen me cry, as well as plenty of strangers and acquaintances. I've been known to cry on the subway and walking down the street—one of my favorite things about living in New York is that people graciously ignore you. I cry upon seeing my favorite works of art—in the Uffizi in front of Botticelli's *Primavera*, I was so moved that I became hysterical, tears streaming down my face, reassuring my concerned friends: *I'm so happy!*

I didn't always love crying. I used to hide it, until hiding became impossible. My cluster headaches would come, so extreme that I would lay shuddering and crying under my sheets, sometimes vomiting or pissing through my tears, and of course when I got them in school I would cry there as well. How humiliating, to start bawling in class for no apparent reason, pretending I had "allergies" and excusing myself to the bathroom to rest my eyes and sob in peace, until I heard the door swing and knew I had to be silent once again.

I'm not sure when my feelings about crying shifted, exactly, but it might have been when I was living with my first girlfriend. When I would start crying in the middle of the night, she would wordlessly wrap me in her arms and hold me until I fell back asleep. When there was no one who hit me or yelled, just people who would rub my back, get me tea, give me a hug, sit with me.

Crying supposedly is a way for the body to release excess cortisol, according to some study they did that shows tears have high amounts of the stress hormone. Cortisol signals to your body that you are in danger: it's the fight/flight/freeze hormone. Crying is a signal that that's over, a release. That's why the body can feel so fresh after a good cry, like you've gotten something out of you, because you have. Crying, much like having an orgasm, is healthy to do on a regular basis. Let it out, let it go, release it. It's okay to cry, really good to cry, healing to cry. Never let anyone tell you otherwise.

Emma Ruth Rundle

(musician, poet, visual artist)

Key

When saved:
a tear of happiness
and thorn too
needling the latter
concludes the recognition
of joy's impermanence
brief well
in time
liquid opal hope
now!
grant my passage
to one late spring's
eternally walled garden
They run in blooms
dew is kept and folded
to be used in despairing hours against the blighting real worlds

Moni Saldaña

(music curator, supervisor & consultant / NRMAL, Turista Universal)

In 2020, I woke up every night in panic about NRMAL, an independent music festival that I was directing. Getting our government-controlled venue (the one we'd been using for the last seven years) was a nightmare because of new rules. Weeks before the festival, I was still uncertain if they were going to cancel us at the last moment. They didn't, but they gave us a curfew of 9 p.m., with no exceptions. We had to make all sorts of adjustments but, in the end, we were happy and convinced ourselves it was for the best.

Flying Lotus was supposed to headline that year, everything was announced. We worked with the team to meet his specific production requests; we had put together a 3-D live show for the first time in Mexico. Festival week came, and I, from the core team of five people, was the only person on-site to do all of the load-in. Between handling all of our vendors and collaborators, emails, phone calls, and messages, I suddenly see an email entitled "IMPORTANT: CANCELLATION." It was from Flying Lotus's agent, stating personal reasons for withdrawing from the festival.

I read it very fast. For a second, I felt myself leave my body. I hid between some bushes and started crying, out of shock. It wasn't just a few tears, it was that sort of panic crying where you breathe heavily. I had no one to talk to and I couldn't let the team that was working there see me in tears, wondering if something was wrong. I won't get into details of the cancellation because that's not the point of this story, but a lot of things happen between getting news like that and making an announcement, because you try, you try to convince his team to come, you check flights, you think of spending money you don't have on a private plane, you get angry and demand a doctor's note, and after all of that back-and-forth you accept the fact and start thinking of how to tell the fans. And you do.

Our office was at a co-workspace where, sometimes, they hosted parties at night. Our space was right on the central patio, and it had a big window with no curtains. So the night before the festival, after being on-site all day, I arrived at our office with the rest of our core team and, while a party was going on literally outside our door, I was inside the office feeling devastated. This cancellation, which was totally out of our control, could potentially jeopardize everything we'd worked for. I started crying again as I read ticket buyers' messages, making fun of me, blaming me, and saying I was scamming them. They were right to be mad, but it's frustrating when they can't know exactly what happened and you become the bad one. Pablo, NRMAL's founder, led me out of the office to talk. In tears, I had to walk between people dancing and partying to make it out of the building. It was all very cinematic now that I think about it. I walked the streets with Pablo that night, crying and just letting it all out. I think it's one of the sweetest moments we've shared, and we've been through a lot.

At this point I sound like a crier who can't control herself, but it just felt like too much. One could assume that after ten years making a festival, things would get easier with time. But in the music industry, that's hardly the case. You try so hard, and you make these crazy decisions, you question yourself and it all becomes personal. It was for me and my team; we left all of ourselves in that project and that's why it's been as successful as it is.

I woke up the next morning, festival day, all swollen, and I felt like I was walking to my funeral. At the festival site, I felt like everyone was looking at me like "poor Moni." I felt observed and ashamed. I didn't want to seem vulnerable to people: because I was the director, because I was in charge, because I was a woman in that position and I was showing my emotions. But I had to be there and give my one thousand percent for the rest of the bands, all the hardworking teams and the fans who decided to attend.

The cancellation led us to change schedules and make another confirmed artist, the Argentinian singer-songwriter Juana Molina, close out the festival. Afterward, I got the most beautiful messages, hugs, words, and vibes from friends, colleagues, fans, and people. The festival happened, the artists were amazing, and Juana Molina gave one of the most special performances I've ever seen. I took the time to watch it all, to enjoy her show front-row, and I couldn't help myself from crying out of happiness while watching her, looking at fans enjoying, seeing the other artists and staff enjoy her show too, dancing, singing, and letting it all sink in: this is why this happened. We didn't need an artist who didn't need NRMAL, we needed an artist who thrived from being there.

My tears evolved from angriness, frustration, helplessness, sadness, realization, hope, happiness, and joy to pure LOVE. I realized that I cry because I care and because I love what I do, because it's not only about me, but about a community of people who care and love too. Music is about connecting, and I was all the way in.

Adam Schatz

(musician, writer, campaigner for quieter music in restaurants)

I *t brings a tear into my eyes, when I begin to realize I've cried so much since you've been gone . . ."*

These words kick off the number, and under Ray Charles's watchful wail the song becomes a quaking devastation, a combustible shuffle that so accurately embodies the silliness of sadness that we can dare to let the endorphins enacted by the music make us so happy while listening to somebody be so sad.

"Drown in My Own Tears" is a song where the entire three and a half minutes could be summed up in four words and save everyone a lot of wasted breath: You Left. I'm Sad. Maybe we can add a fifth word: boohoo.*

You left, I'm sad, boohoo.

I suppose that's what makes music so wonderful. No one really wants to hear you yap about how bad you feel for more than thirty seconds. But if you sing it? That buys you some time. And if you can sing it well? Well . . . you could probably make a whole career outta that.

*Let's make a pledge. If this book sells more than one hundred copies, we all have to get boohoo *tattooed on our knuckles.*

And sure, something can be said for poetry, the repetitive stretch of a deep feeling beyond the time permitted. But this song isn't just expressive linguistics. It's a plea. A beg. A dramatic cry for attention. And that drama is what makes the song all the more accurate. Sadness and pain rock us in exactly that manner, taking a hammer that should logically only cause a snippet of hurt, and instead making the sorrow last well beyond reason. A logic-free free fall into woe and drudge. When you are sad, there's no stopping that tumble. There's no convincing yourself that life goes on and pain gets less painful, even though past encounters have often proven that to be true. So what else is there to do? You cry to the one who left you, you dig your heels deep into the linoleum, and you say something you know isn't true, just to get a response. *I guess I'll drown in my own tears.*

That'll show you. That'll show everybody.

With a little distance, sure, it's immature. With a little resolve, of course, I didn't drown. But did you hear how well I sang it? Pretty good, right? Please . . . come on home?

Sam Schrader

(social studies and English teacher)

have two stories that stick out, one about a high schooler and one about a middle schooler. The high school story centers around one of the star players on our school's football team. He and I had a good rapport, but I know a lot of other teachers found him frustrating. The spring of his junior year, I catch him plagiarizing an entire paper on *The Great Gatsby*. When I confront him about the paper, his jovial disposition disappears and this six-six teenager just breaks down sobbing. He admits to plagiarism and says he got so far behind in his work that he cheated as a last resort. I try my best to comfort him, saying how sometimes we fall into cutting corners rather than asking a teacher for grace. Still crying, he says that his biggest worries are his parents and not getting into a D-1 football program. He just unraveled in my classroom for about forty minutes. I helped him muster up the courage to own up to cheating to his parents and assured him that this wasn't going to ruin his life. The nice ending to the story is that he currently *is* a D-1 college football player. I had never seen a high schooler, an embodiment of every football stereotype, turn into a scared boy right in front of my eyes.

The middle school story involves a very sweet but very nerdy seventh-grade boy. This was at the beginning of the school year and when I shifted from teaching high school to middle school. Our school district has two elementary schools that feed into one middle school after sixth grade. Apparently, this boy was being teased by a group of students from a different elementary school. Middle schoolers are effective at bullying, and they managed to bring up both his DnD nerdiness and that he was from a lower socioeconomic level than them. (One elementary school had a "rich" reputation; the other had a "poor" reputation.) This student walked into my classroom with his head fully slumped over like Charlie Brown walking home. I ask him what's wrong and he looks up at me with his eyes full of tears and asks me why rich kids are such jerks. I get up from my desk, trying to think of what to say, and just as I'm about to speak, he sits on an adjacent desk and begins to sob. It then quickly turns into crying about being called a nerd, about feeling so self-conscious for crying in front of me, and being frustrated about being misunder-

stood. I tried my best to comfort him with all the teacher platitudes about courage and that it's okay to cry, but I found myself tearing up a bit because I saw so much of me in this kid. I was that same kid when I was twelve.

Scherezade Siobhan

(psychologist, writer, educator, community catalyst, gardener of roses,
founded/runs Qureist, a therapeutic space for psychosocial wellness)

The first time B speaks about her inability to cry after starting
antidepressants, the streets of Mumbai are angling for space on
the list of most water-logged places, somewhere between Atlantis
and Venice. Water has been spilling over into the streets with a bull-
ish vagrancy. We are sitting in the breakout space of my office, close
to the window where translucent threads of rain unfurl across the
pane. We watch throngs ten floors down scuttling about like a co-
terie of marbles, each person tumbling toward their own chaotic
direction.

B was diagnosed with clinical depression about a year ago and
initiating medication has been a reluctant wrangle at best. She fears
the shadowy revolving door of history. Her father fought the needling dissonance of the same condition she now faces, and, in her
own words, she saw him go from a buoyant humorist to an "emp-
tied wine bottle" following trials with voluntary psychiatric con-
finement. It is hard to calibrate free will with repression. It is hard
to harmonize the sour notes that deck the edges of our conversations
as she laughs and lets "like father, like daughter" slowly slip from

under her breath. B has an expressed disdain for the false equiva-
lence between tears and rain which reminds me of a quote I saw
once: "The tears are looking for a place to alight in, they aren't rain
/ they're desolation."

B seconds that summary with her own analysis: "I like rains.
Monsoon reminds me of our capacity to endure and release without
holding on. Rains are about unmooring—a freedom I am distant
from when I feel depressed. The only other place where I find this
simultaneous expression of freedom and flight at the same time is
inside a book and, more so, in poems."

In *Crying: The Natural and Cultural History of Tears*, Tom Lutz
recounts how the earliest written records of crying—the Ras Shamra
texts—were discovered on Canaanite clay tablets dating from the
fourteenth century BC in present-day Syria. They belonged to the
ancient city of Ugarit, which was consumed by an earthquake. One
of the fragments tells the story of the virgin goddess Anat, the sister of Ba'al, as she hears the news of his death. Quite naturally, she
weeps at the news. The accepted scholarly translation is that Anat
"continued sating herself with weeping, to drink tears
like wine." This, the earliest mention of tears in history,
suggests that they are induced by grief, and that they
offer satiety, even a kind of intoxication.

In a purely scientific classification,
there are three types of tears—basal, or
tears that help lubricate the cornea; reflex,
or the kind of tears that occur as response
to physical irritation (onions, anyone?); and
psychic or emotional, the tears that are linked
to feelings, cognition, and expression. But crying has its own cultural, social, and religious
connotations that stretch far and wide.

"Moral weeping" was once differentiated from regular, "physical" crying as an expression of authentic sadness. Religions have often equated penance with crying. Certain cultures including Korea and India even have the tradition of employing "official criers" at funerals to indicate the social significance of the deceased. In literature, Beckett once proclaimed that "the tears of the world are a constant quantity" and in "Requiem: Epilogue," Anna Akhmatova quickens the lyrical pulse when she writes, "From my eyelids, bronze, unmoving, may snowflakes fall like tears, melting."

B, like many other clients of mine who had recently started antidepressants, felt a certain emotional paralysis once the meds kicked in and she was unable to cry. A week after our session, B texts me a Woolf quote that reads, "Now let us issue from the darkness of solitude." Accompanying this text is an emoji that looks like it's crying from one side and smiling from the other.

Curtis Santiago

(artist, poonie papa)

W hy are you crying?" she asked as she entered the nest. My tears defied gravity, flowing back up my cheeks with each upward bounce on the exercise ball/slumber machine. "Because, because he will never be as small as he is right now, he will never fit in the space between my wrist and elbow pit again." My milk-breathed, mouth-breathing, little Nerf football of a human.

At that moment, with the grayish-blue afternoon sunlight warming us, I'm hyperaware that with every beat of his tiny baby body drum, he dances a little bit further away from needing his poonie papa the way he needs his poonie papa right now. I'm JOYvastated. I'm ripped open. And I'm in a love bubble like I've never known. The water comes, knowing it will flood my eyes again for first steps, first colds, first kisses, and first goodbyes. You come from a long line of male criers.

Jordan Sondler

(artist, author)

I was barely ten when my dad pulled my friend Nate aside and promised to loan him his Porsche if he took me to the prom.

In reality, many years passed before my romantic entanglements transcended beyond AIM and into the three-dimensional world, certainly long after my dad's death. College opened up new doors— men with facial hair and tattoos, and folks who hadn't known me all their lives as the weird girl who loved to collect snail shells and oak leaves.

One thing remained constant in my transition to young adulthood: my gravitation toward conditional affection. I sought it out like a security blanket. Something was so familiar, and almost comforting, about receiving the "worm in the apple" version of everything. For so many reasons—my body, my depression, my general strangeness—I stood out. And when you're different you are lucky to get what you get, right?

Thus began an era of giving with lack of discernment. Giving my body, my emotions, my energy. To a man who was comfortable enough to pour a beer on my head while we flirted, to a friend who crawled into my bed to touch me and never talk about it again.

And then there was Max: someone I admired from a distance, and once we knew each other it was immediately more. If you squinted, our dynamic appeared normal—dates to see a movie or a band—but up close there were so many holes. I didn't dare ask what we were doing. I didn't dare ask why we had never kissed but engaged physically in things that seemed far more intimate. I was riding a wave and I was too afraid to ask where it'd drop me off. I knew this situation, similar to the others I'd experienced, was deeply flawed.

When Max decided it was time for someone new, a petite and abrasive girl whose friendship was foisted upon me months prior, I was not surprised. When my friends had to beg him to tell me, threatening to do me the kindness if he didn't, I was not surprised. And when I never heard from Max again, I was not surprised.

Although this was just another self-fulfilling prophecy, something finally broke inside of me. I could no longer be a vessel for this endless pit of self-loathing. I had come to expect so little from others, but least of all myself. I needed to find a way back to the little girl who didn't always expect less, who didn't expect dysfunction.

I took a shower that night and cried and ached. I was overcome with nausea and disgust in a way I had never experienced, and still have never again to this day. I remember that slimy, awful feeling of disappointment like it was yesterday—my skin crawled out of shame. I was finally coming head-to-head with the hatred I'd harbored for myself for so goddamn long. And the air was finally being let out of the tires. Enough was enough.

Lauren Spear

(musician, writer, performs as Le Ren, very tall)

To cry is to experience release. I am so grateful to shed emotion through my eyeballs, and to let sadness or pain or joy spill over. In writing this, I'm realizing I don't know where tear water comes from. Is there a little water tower located somewhere in the head that is waiting to be drained? Also, can sea mammals cry underwater? Maybe they do, but their tears mix with the ocean and they don't even know it's happening? I have some googling to do. What I do know is that the human body is made up of sixty percent water, so it makes sense to me that the water that I am becomes visible when I need proof of what I'm feeling inside. I can feel it on my cheeks, wipe it on my sleeve, or lick it up and put it right back where it came from.

Here is a song I wrote with my friend Jonah Yano called "The Water That I Am."

The Water That I Am

I've been filling up
On the water that I was
And the water that I am
(The water that I am)
I put the River in my mouth
And I let it all drain out
Just to try and understand

The water that I was
The water that I am
The water that I was
And the water that I am

Aren't we all wells of memories felt?
Can you see water run deep?
If you keep it safe then I might let you trace
The shape of the water in me

I've been washing up
In the water that I was
And the water that I am
(The water that I am)
Now I close my mouth and wait
For my form to sublimate
I begin to understand

The water that I was
(The water that I was)
And the water that I am
(The water that I am)

Ramesh Srivastava

(musician, writer)

My friend Eugene once said that when we are stuck in our minds and searching for answers, it often leads to discombobulation and exhaustion. He believed that all we need to do in these moments is conjure the memory of something funny or moving, and instantly we are reconnected with the inherent wisdom of the heart. Many times throughout my life, when I have felt overwhelmed or at a logistical impasse, I've sat with songs that I love ("Let It Be," "Into My Arms," "Stand by Me") and allowed them to move me to tears. Every time, this has given me the perspective and peace I need to make a clear decision.

For a while I considered a career shift from rock & roll to therapy, but despite my efforts to move in this direction I found myself continually pulled back to my first and greatest love: music. It was during this time that I began thinking about what I call the "spiritual value of entertainment." I theorize that the reason human beings are so drawn to music and movies—and perhaps all forms of art—is that, in a world that places a lot of value on surface-level behavior, they provide momentary access to something more real or visceral, a dip into the ineffable meaningfulness of life.

Whether it is a love song, a banging techno track, a tear-jerking drama, or a screwball comedy, the experience takes us out of our minds and back home to our hearts, the laughter and tears providing a wordless answer to the eternal one-word question: Why? For at least a moment we don't wonder why we are here, we just *are*. I wrote a poem about this a few years ago. It goes like this:

How many kids get guitars for Christmas and dream of escape?

    Escape into their own dreams

To burn at the fusion point

Mama lives in the floating world, Papa lives in the world of hard truths

Both are equally important

I'm backstage, waiting for the minor to turn major

Searching for the god in entertainment

        There is god in laughter

        There is god in tears

        There is god in lifting the veil

Eric Steuer

(writer, musician/occasional rapper)

I don't think of myself as someone who eats a lot of fast food, but I've just done some back-of-the-napkin math and there's zero chance that I've been to the Taco Bell in our area any less than one hundred times. I should probably stop blaming COVID for making me feel so sad and gross all the time.

I've never actually been inside this particular TB location—it's always crowded and has a tiny parking lot, so I just do the drive-through. No matter what time of day it is, there's a long line of cars, many of them driven by people like me: midforties, exhausted, waiting for something quick and cheap to stuff into their faces. The line is ingeniously designed so that once your car's bumper has crossed even the backmost part of the stretch, you're barricaded on either side with cement curbs that keep you from turning around or backing out. You're forced to stick with your regrettable decision.

Over the past few months, there's been a new guy taking orders. He is young and has long hair tucked under his company-issued dad cap. He's stressed, fastidious, and almost embarrassingly polite—it seems like this must be his first job. He's got to be putting in a lot of hours, because he's there about ninety percent of the time I visit. You can tell who it is before you roll up to the window and see him in person, because he starts each interaction through the menu board's talk box the same way: "I'm very sorry about the wait. I hope that it wasn't too much of an inconvenience." Verbatim, every time.

Yesterday I stopped by to pick up my regular haul of two bean burritos, no onions, no red sauce, and six packets of Fire sauce. The young guy delivered his usual spiel through the speaker, but this time, his voice, which is normally inflected with sincere concern about the delay that Mexican Pizza's popularity causes customers, indicated that something was wrong. He was stifling tears.

"No problem at all, man." I cringed lightly as the last word came out of my mouth, but I hoped "man" made it clear that I was one of the good guys in this world. "It wasn't even that long of a wait."

I drove forward to pay and accept my bag of salt and oily carbs. His eyes were red, and he sniffled behind a cloth mask that had the logo of the area's biggest hospital group printed across the front. I considered asking him what was going on, whether everything was okay, but I worried that calling attention to his crying would make him feel ashamed.

"That'll be $3.70." I assumed he'd made a mistake, since my order always comes out to just over four dollars, but I decided not to push it since he was in a bad place. Whatever was in the bag would probably be fine anyway. He ran my credit card and handed off my food. "Thanks for choosing Taco Bell." I pulled out of the drive-through, parked on the side of the road, and looked at the receipt to find that he'd given me the restaurant's senior discount.

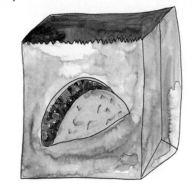

Brandon Stosuy

(editor of this book)

I saw a guy shoveling snow and crying.
And a guy looking at bulk almonds in Whole Foods and crying.
Passed a guy hurriedly eating a piece of pizza and crying.
Guy with fidget spinner crying.
Guy in Merge Records shirt crying.
Saw a guy at a urinal checking his phone and crying . . .
and another in a JFK bathroom crying to Chicago's "Hard for Me
    to Say I'm Sorry."
Guy with a mohawk eating fruit salad and crying.
Guy biting a sandwich and crying.
Crust punk on the subway reading a John Irving novel and crying.
When you make eye contact with someone crying on the subway
    and instinctively mouth, *I'm so sorry.*
saw a guy crying on his hoverboard
guy crying outside a vape shop
I once saw a guy moshing and crying at the same time.
Just saw a guy looking at a photo of biscuits on his phone and
    crying
Guy in art supply store crying

to the goth guy i saw earlier air-drumming and crying: i'm here for
   you.
guy reading kombucha bottle label and crying
guy moshing and crying
guy at Iceage show crying
guy in barfight crying
guy vaping and crying
guy playing the Strokes loudly on his phone, crying
guy crying during Lightning Bolt
guy listening to Deafheaven and crying
guy with "Optimism" canvas bag crying
report from Barcelona: guy in Deicide shirt crying
guy with Skinny Puppy t-shirt crying.
guy in red and black plaid shirt crying
guy in DON'T WORRY BE HAPPY t-shirt crying.
guy in Ministry hoodie crying.
guy drinking Arizona Iced Tea crying.
guy crying in the cereal aisle
guy eating beef jerky and crying
guy drinking oat milk crying
saw two guys high-five and then break down crying.
saw a guy beatboxing and crying
guy eating a grilled cheese sandwich and crying.
saw a guy look at his corn muffin and then start crying.
guy jogging, crying
guy trying to log in to gmail, crying.
guy hitting send on an email and crying
guy crying while apologizing
Lyft driver listening to My Chemical Romance and crying.
Lyft driver listening to Future, chugging water, and crying.
Lyft driver listening to "I Took a Pill in Ibiza" and crying

saw guy in the airport typing over and over on his phone while
  crying.

guy in Joy Division shirt looking at his cell phone as he walks,
  crying

guy listening to Blues Traveler's "Run-Around" on a small
  portable radio and crying.

guy humming Gin Blossoms' "Hey Jealousy," crying.

on some level, this guy singing and crying along to Coldplay in the
  salsa aisle makes sense to me.

I was at a kid's birthday party today where a guy did an acoustic
  cover of "Sweet Child O' Mine," and some people started
  crying.

passed a guy on the street carrying an econo-size package of toilet
  paper and crying.

saw a guy doing his grocery shopping in CVS and crying.

guy with goatee crying

guy drinking seltzer crying

guy doing karaoke crying

life coach crying

saw a guy with his face painted green
  crying

saw a guy crying at an all-you-
  can-eat buffet in Mexico.

guy on subway telling friend
  "sharks die if they stop
  swimming" suddenly
  starts to cry.

guy in the grocery store
  staring at bags of
  potato chips and
  crying.

overheard: "not a great day to cry yourself to sleep, bro."
saw a guy say "swag" to a friend and then
    start crying.
when someone says
    they're "screaming"
    online, but you
    look across the
    room and they're
    crying into their
    cold brew.
when you wave at
    someone you think you
    know then realize they're
    looking past you, and the
    look on their face is sad, and
    soon you're both crying.

A friend texted me this morning.

friend: i was crying. were you talking about me?

me: i was talking about all of us.

Henry Stosuy

(middle schooler, son of this book's editor)

I cried when we got the message that school was canceled during the start of the pandemic. I cried because it was my second-to-final year of elementary school and I knew I would never see a lot of those kids again.

Jake Stosuy

(fourth grader, son of this book's editor)

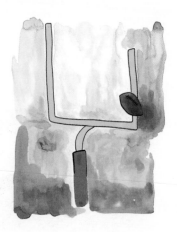

I cried when the Buffalo Bills lost to the Kansas City Chiefs
because it was so FREAKING close and it's like I got four
numbers in the lottery but worse I cried myself to sleep
what happened was the Bills were losing by four touchdowns
then the Bills came back with Josh Allen throwing four
touchdowns then Tyler Bass kicked a field goal then the Chiefs

were blocked then Gabriel Davis scored a touchdown then

Tyreek Hill of the Chiefs scored a touchdown then it went to overtime

the Chiefs got the ball in overtime and scored then what

happened was I cried myself to sleep then later they

CHANGED the overtime rule.

Todd Stosuy

(field services manager, Santa Cruz County Animal Shelter, brother of this book's editor)

I haven't cried in almost seven years, but I make people cry almost every day. I am an animal law enforcement officer. One of my responsibilities is making death notifications when someone's dog or cat is hit by a car, is killed by another animal, or dies by some other manner. I know how a face can go from smiling to clenching up and then ultimately to crying, sobbing, and mumbling in disbelief. I can't hug these people. It's not allowed. I just stand there. I carry tissues in my pocket and give them as a comfort. The simple gesture seems to give them some solace. I've learned that saying "I know how you feel" or "I am sorry for your loss" does little to comfort people. I've had a few individuals shout that I cannot understand how they feel or how can I be sorry for the loss of their pet?

So, I just stand there and offer a tissue. No one has ever yelled at me when taking the tissue. The last time I cried was when my eighteen-year-old dog died. At the time, I wish someone would have offered me a tissue.

Erin A. Sulla

(librarian)

I've always been scared of death. Of growing old, decaying, disappearing. So, naturally, in the summer after my first year of college, I landed a job in deathcare.

My duties were often detached from the realities of the industry. I spent my days in a nondescript office answering the phone. People called me from all over the country with important but often innocuous questions, asking about TSA guidelines for transporting ashes or inquiring about pre-need plans—the logistics of death rather than the complicated humanity of it.

However, every few weeks, I would receive an emotional phone call—someone calling from their sibling's funeral, a person planning their parent's final days. As the weeks passed and I fell into a routine, I negotiated a tentative truce with death.

One morning, I picked up the phone and rattled off my standard greeting. I heard suppressed sobs from the other side.

"I'm at the hospital. I didn't know who to call," the man choked out. And then, the worst sentence anyone could possibly say: "Our baby just died."

How do you respond to that? How do you reconcile that

sentence—that horrible, horrible sentence—with the warm summer sun shining through dusty blinds? There I sat, freshly nineteen years old, surrounded by a scattered constellation of sticky notes, a teetering tower of pamphlets I needed to mail, and scribbled lists of contact information for state mortuary boards. It all seemed so ridiculous, so insignificant, in a world where the joyful anticipation of new parenthood could crumble under the suffocating injustice of such loss.

"I don't know what to do. I need to know where to cremate my baby."

As part of my onboarding, I learned that ashes consisted of charred bone fragments. Everything else—skin, hair, organs—burned away in the process. To a lapsed Catholic—even one still wary of death—it felt perfectly natural: ashes to ashes, dust to dust.

There was one caveat, my coworkers told me. Cremation needs bones to turn to ash. You can cremate a deceased infant, but sometimes, especially for fetuses without substantial bones, there could be little if any human remains left afterward.

I wanted to reverse time: to never pick up that phone, never learn what cremation was, never take this job. But as the man cried, I offered him reassurance and sympathy. After a few minutes, I knew I needed to pass on his call to someone who could explain, if needed, the difficult reality of cremation. I transferred him to my supervisor, and never heard from him again. In all the emotion, I never even learned his name.

I'm still afraid of death. Of decay and oblivion and lost legacies. But after that summer in deathcare, I feel more prepared to confront it, almost as if those phone calls forged an armor against my fear. And sometimes, in the quiet of night, I return to that moment, where all that mattered to a grieving father was that someone picked up the phone. Someone listened. Someone heard his tears.

Daniel Tam-Claiborne

(multiracial author and essayist, rice enthusiast)

It was the kind of movie theater that didn't have a marquee. Grand Avenue Cinemas was located on a dismal stretch of Long Island, sandwiched unceremoniously between a liquor store and a Dollar Tree. The four of us had driven there from Jones Beach, the sun waning in the sky, on the kind of perfect summer day that seemed to signal that the summer was coming to an end.

Scott and Julie—my two best friends in the world—were up in the front seats. I'd known them both since middle school, and though we'd all left New York for different colleges, we'd always managed to come back home for the summers, carrying on like we'd never left. No summer was this truer than 2010—the August after graduation—when we were back in the city, waiting for the Great Recession to pass and for our lives, as we'd been promised, to change.

In a few days, they would. The three of us would be leaving New York again, only this time more permanently. We'd landed jobs in other cities, found roommates, paid security deposits on new apartments. It felt like being on the precipice of something great and thrilling. There would be no more school breaks and no certainty about the next time we'd see each other. The day at Jones Beach, followed by a night out on the Lower East Side, would be our last hurrah—the end of this chapter of our friendship as we knew it—and we vowed to savor it for as long as we could.

Only, I'd taken a hacksaw to the plan. Sitting next to me in the back of Julie's car was Rachel, a sophomore from my college whom I'd developed a crush on. We'd flirted for weeks over text before I convinced Julie to pick her up from the PATH train that morning. The black one-piece she'd worn to the beach clung effortlessly to her body. Her hair was a cascade of dark curls that Scott would later compare to Medusa. Reaching across the back seat, Rachel pressed her hand against mine, the gloss of her suntan lotion making her arms glisten.

Rachel wasn't twenty-one, so the bar idea was out. Scott offered a hookah lounge that didn't card that we used to frequent in high school. I suggested somewhere dark and quiet instead. Julie and Scott were no fools. We'd pulled these kinds of stunts before—privileging flings over friendship—but never when the stakes were this high. Still, though I could sense their disappointment, neither of them called me on it. When we finally got to the theater, Scott and Julie lit up a pair of cloves in the parking lot, and Rachel and I went inside.

The lobby reeked of stale butter. The carpet was a shade of maroon so deep we could only speculate at its last cleaning. We didn't even know what was playing, so I chose the movie with the closest showtime. *Toy Story 3* would be the kind of movie we wouldn't be tempted to pay attention to. It had been over a decade since I'd seen the original and I felt no more regard for Buzz and Woody and the gang than I did for anyone who would spoil a last opportunity with Rachel.

The opening should have convinced me otherwise. A buoyant

montage of Andy as a young boy playing with his toys fades out to the clipped Randy Newman lyric "our friendship will never die." We learn that Andy, now seventeen, is leaving to go to college. All his toys but Woody will soon be relegated to his parents' attic. Sitting next to Rachel, I felt my heart jump. What had once been his most important confidants in the world were suddenly barely more than an afterthought. I felt the betrayal in my bones. I tried to hide the tears in the corners of my eyes.

The rest of the movie proved only more devastating. Woody and the gang end up on a landfill conveyor belt that leads to an incinerator. In what appears to be their dying moments, the toys wordlessly express their love for each other, accepting the end of their lives as I felt my own adolescence going up in flames around me.

In the movie's final scene, Andy donates his toys to a neighborhood girl named Bonnie. He introduces each one to her and is surprised to find Woody at the bottom of the box. Although initially hesitant, he passes him on to Bonnie along with the others. For a few precious moments, Andy is not a young man about to go to college. He is running around in Bonnie's backyard with Woody on his shoulders, just like he did all those years ago. Driving away from the house, Andy seems to make peace in a way that I still hadn't: that moving on means being willing to let go.

The tears flowed with abandon. I brought my own hand from Rachel's armrest to my face.

"They're just toys," she said, when the credits rolled. "Kids' stuff."

I nodded, choking back tears. I couldn't tell her that, deep down, I was each one of those scared toys, staring down the fiery inferno of adulthood. Without really knowing how it happened, my friends and I had grown up, trading our innocence for a shot at the world. Only, it all felt so sudden. No matter how long we'd known this time was coming, there was no good way to prepare for it.

I stood up after the credits and turned toward the exit, where Scott and Julie had been sitting. Letting go, mourning the past, acceptance. It all seemed so infuriatingly out of reach. But perhaps, then, it didn't have to be that way. Was it possible to grow up and not let go? To move on but still remember? If we could look back on our fondest memories and allow them to be part of our core being, we could go forward without abandoning the past. Like the toys' new lives with Bonnie, ours would not just be an ending but a beginning too.

When I saw Scott and Julie, their eyes were bleary, faces red. I could sense they felt it too. Whatever came after wouldn't be the same, but it didn't have to be. Without saying a word, we smiled at each other and bounded, sobbing and exultant, into each other's arms.

Erin Taylor

(author of Bimboland*, writer)*

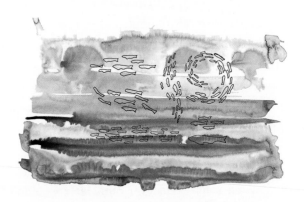

Stray dog 4 Stray dog

we stare at one another, in mirror, in face,
    birds staring at a horizon at the break of day

        it took me a long time to know the formation
    my mouth takes saying

        "I need you to tell me you want me!"

how odd, how deeply insatiable I have become
      not because of you, even though
      you are wonderful, darling, bright even

yet in life itself I have become insatiable, nothing can sate
        what is not asked
     what is not recognized
            I have been
            a stray dog
            and unless
            you leave
            food for
            me
            I don't return
I BEG YOU TO LEAVE
THE WATER BOWL
FULL, I OFTEN THIRST

I second-guess best intentions
        bridges collapse with best intentions
      structural precarity be damned
      I will find ways to be,
    to be loved is not my concern anymore
    I am deeply embedded in myself now

I forget time, I dream of the blank state
      of your eyes in the mirror
smoking in the hammerstein ballroom
      I naturally occur

the moonlight crisp
touches you without asking as you cry
in the jumpy house of childhood desires
we always race to our pasts
especially as there is no future
yet so much to atone for

Brent Thomas

(hospice bereavement counselor)

Crying is my job.

If you meet me at work, it's because death has crossed your path. There's a likelihood that one or both of us will cry by the end of our call.

Tears are the currency of relationships.

Tears are the cost of loss.

Tears are the currency of our relationship.

It's always the same. Everyone apologizes. As if crying is something to hide or be ashamed of rather than the flow of grief, the river of our love. The best I can do is hold space; safe space; nonjudgmental space; space to say what needs to be said or feel what must be felt.

Sometimes it's a quiet sob that wilts in the space between. Sometimes it's a rumble or a wail and sometimes it's blubbering. Crying can be ugly. No one wants to be ugly, and no one wants to hurt. But the only way through grief is to grieve.

As a hospice bereavement counselor:

I am a heart with ears.

I am a repository of tears.

We cry at separation; but tears can also bring us together. Crying is sacred space. Perhaps someday we'll meet there. I'll have the tissues ready.

Lindsay Thomaston

(writer, photographer)

The first job to offer me a stab at adulthood (health insurance) was one of those *we're a family here* workplaces. I grew up in an unstable household and I ferociously avoid conversation with relatives that attempts any vulnerability greater than small talk. So, to me, the job was, in fact, like family.

Small talk revolves around the weather, so working the water-cooler with coworkers is especially easy in a state like Georgia, where the forecast spans at least four different climates in a typical week. On the rare occasion that it's been Too Normally With Rain or Too Normally Without, coworkers might, however, be inspired to pry a bit deeper, for instance: *Are you in school for this?* "No, out," I'd say. "And not for this." You can imagine the puzzled look that would follow when I'd say, "Actually," hands shuffling a fresh battery into the bottom of a digital camera, "I have a degree in politics." They'd give me that woeful gaze that says, *Sad, we thought gifted children might have more tricks in them.* We really were a family here.

"I want people to think of us as the Disney World of school photography," my CEO once said, waving his hands about like his fingers were clutching at an invisible martini glass. I had friends who worked at Disney. "Underpaid," they reported. "But healthcare!" they'd add.

There was no Main Street, U.S.A. at my company, nor were there any glass slippers or mouse-shaped pastries. What there was in common with Disney World was sweeping away the criers from the floor. It was imperative to the guest experience that a graduating senior's photo session maintain an unblemished sense of phantasmic celebration. After hours of primping, preening, and posing, I'd relinquish my sentimental clients to the sales team, where they'd be led down a corridor of graduates that came before; this corridor, winding away from the public nosiness of our bustling studio floor, led to an array of private rooms where the lights were dimmed to a welcoming glow. Inside, an oil diffuser puffed out deep breaths of calming lavender. "Have a snack," the sales rep would say, gesturing to an assortment of chips and granola on the coffee table before them. Then they'd gesture to the fine print, making certain that the parents understood the four-figure price of the session they'd just completed. Sometimes you'd pass by a room at this exact moment and it'd sound like a B-movie operating room with all the screaming and all the crying. Out on the studio floor, the triumphant celebration of graduates continued, a parade of parents and teens thinking about complimentary cups of Keurig coffee and not of fine print.

Once, I photographed a girl I was certain was one mall visit away from being scouted. She had that sort of face that sells yogurt or sunscreen or silk blouses, all freckles and warmth. "You look really fat when you stand like that," came her mom's voice before I'd even released my finger from the shutter. Mom came closer, turned toward me, then to her daughter, then back to me. "Doesn't she? When she stands like that?" I thought she looked like she might sell me yogurt. The child gave me sorry eyes and I gave them back. "I think you look very nice," I told the girl. "Just go ahead and exhale

and make sure you aren't carrying any tightness in your shoulders."
I raised the camera to take another photo. "Hold on," said Mom.
The child's face fell in my viewfinder. "I think her hair is too flat,
you know? And she needs to suck it in, she's still looking totally
bloated." This continued for some time, the child's hair being too
flat, then too big, then too frizzy, her
shoes too casual, too fancy. Not to
mention she was fat. "You need
to smile confidently, you're
looking very unsure," said Mom.
"Well, I can't imagine why,"
sputtered the daughter, her
resolve finally spilling into
a defeated fit. I disappeared
for a moment to bring them tis-
sues and green tea but when I returned, they
had already been vanished from the floor. "They've decided to re-
schedule," informed a sales rep from over my shoulder.

The one that burns most in my brain was the single mom who
came in with two daughters: one, the graduate star, the other, six,
maybe seven. Some of my clients were champions of small talk, stoic
ice blocks finding newfangled ways to comment on the weather.
Others were ready to give me their life story. My favorites were
the ice blocks who would melt, the ones who began with reserva-
tion before warming into a comfortable cadence with me. When
these ones melted, we talked about hip-hop and whether the eldest
daughter, the graduate, preferred oils to watercolors. Mom boasted
about what a standout her daughter was in choir and how she could
pull off an Alicia Keys solo like nobody's business. We all lauded
Lauryn Hill and debated whether or not a biopic could do Glo-
ria Estefan justice. The youngest darted between our legs while we

joked, pausing occasionally to tell her older sister how pretty she looked in her photos. "It was a little hard to take off from work, but I'm glad we all got to come today," said the mom. "This has really been so fun."

As the session neared its close, the graduate slipped on her cap and gown for the final pictures. Mom pressed her hand to her chest as if her heart would fall out from between her ribs if she didn't hold it in place. I watched her gaze fill up like a dunk tank. "Her father passed away earlier this year," said the mom, shuffling around in her bag.

She located a tissue-wrapped bundle and began undoing the layers of paper.

"It's been really hard, you know, with *everything*. But here she is. She made it. I know he's so proud of her." She handed me a picture frame. Inside was the image of a man, smiling. "I was wondering if she could hold this for one of the photos so that they can have a photo together, in her graduation gown." I passed the girl the photo of her father and raised my camera. Mom clutched her chest again. "You look so smart and pretty!" said the little sister, dancing circles around my tripod. "She does look very pretty," I agreed, and then I watched as they were escorted down the hall and into the deep breaths of lavender.

Kate Thompson

(psychotherapist)

I watch people cry almost every day. Tears from disappointment, anger, loss. Tears from the pain of losing one's childhood innocence to an adult's cruel and critical voice. Tears from joy. Tears from failure. Prior to the pandemic, I would order my tissues in bulk. Now I watch people across the screen wipe their tears with whatever they have handy—paper towels, their shirts, but usually their hands.

Occasionally, my clients' tears will connect with something deeper within me. I think of one client who came to me the day after her mother died. Seeing her at the beginning of her own journey in grief reminded me of my own twenty-year journey. I felt for her and the lifelong pain she will experience, anticipating a sense of absence in both the day-to-day moments and in the big events life brings. Tears welled up in my eyes for a moment as she sobbed into her fistful of tissues. While psychotherapists do our best to not let the hurt sides of ourselves appear as we're showing up for others, sometimes connection means showing something we at times try to keep on the inside.

Walter Thompson-Hernández

(writer-director)

'Ve seen my mom and aunts cry eleven times in the past two years. The sight of the coffin is always the catalyst, prompting a supple memory, perhaps a familiar scent. When their fingertips reach for the dark mahogany wood, tiny lakes of liquid—filled with proteins, salt, and fatty acids—crystalize under their eyes. Tia Licha is the quietest crier in the group. She gently leans into her right shoulder to sob, the way people sometimes do when attempting to quell a nagging cough. My mom, the youngest of the three, looks around the room, searching for other pairs of eyes—maybe it's validation she seeks, maybe it's something else. She reminds me of the way a small child looks after they've scraped their knee on the ground: a split second usually decides whether the child will cry or not. A split second decides whether or not my mom will cry, too. Tia Meche's tears, the oldest sister, reminds me of someone who once had a lot of money and

lost it all after a series of poor decisions. Her tears are full of shame and, most of all, regret—like someone who knows they should have cried while the person they are mourning was still alive. Eleven times in the past two years. I hope they cry less in the next. I hope I cry less, too.

Jia Tolentino

(writer)

A few days before I gave birth to my first child in August 2020, I started crying, and didn't stop for approximately eight to ten weeks. The tears were as disorienting as the arrival of the baby—before this, I'd cried once, maybe twice a year—but they were also, strangely, a line back in time to my previous self, a person who cried most easily when doing something like acid, overwhelmed by a kind of shimmery existential gratitude that always seemed firmly predicated on transience, absurdity, and loss. The baby-induced tears mostly came from the same place. (A couple of drained-to-the-bone fights with my boyfriend, Andrew, were the exception—one of which occurred after he took a photo of the baby in a cute outfit and proudly sent it to his entire family, failing to see that her backdrop was my entire, distended, naked boob.) Even before the baby arrived, I felt the shattering, contradictive delicacy that she would bring to my sense of time in the early months—the sweet and awful endlessness of each afternoon, the grinding inexorability of the trials of the future, the vanishing snapshots of each of us as we were for just a moment, Andrew's serious face as he painted my toenails before I went into labor, the two of us cramming bagel sandwiches into our mouths while the days-old baby slept between us, the sunny morning we took our first shaky walk to the park. When the baby was on my chest, it was exactly like I was tripping: if there was music playing, or if the light was slanted at a certain angle, I instantly burst into tears. I sobbed, feeling like a big old dog with a velvety puppy, the first time we figured out breastfeeding when she was eleven days old. I cried when I realized we were managing—that we were all okay—and when I thought about what this would be like without money to pay for diapers or without friends leaving cookies and hand-me-downs on our doorstep. I cried from sludgy anger, too, a sense that I was being leeched of all intelligence and sharpness, and guilt that I felt overwhelmed when we had all the luck and love in the world. *It might never get better than this*, I thought, one day, flooded with terror and sweetness, tears welling up while I watched the baby watch butterflies flit through a bush.

Noelia Towers

(visual artist)

find it fascinating how the reasons for crying change throughout the years. When you're a newborn, you cry while experiencing discomfort or when your physiological needs aren't met. We learn that crying attracts the attention of a caregiver who will bring us relief. However, as we age and become self-sufficient, the emotions that lead to crying start to shift. I find myself crying less often, but I do find myself less and less able to control when, where, and why: tears of happiness while watching a movie; tears of joy after a wholesome interaction with a stranger on the street; tears of frustration and anger after an asinine argument; unstoppable tears after a long, heartfelt hug with a family member, friend, or significant other. Sometimes we don't know when waterworks will come out, and the purest thing is to let the tears flow, to truly cleanse the soul. I have witnessed my grandfather—a callous, bold, insensitive man who grew up during the civil war in Spain and lived through a thirty-six-year dictatorship in an era when men weren't supposed to let their feelings show—suddenly become soft, emotional, and empathetic after the passing of my grandmother. Life comes full circle; we complete the cycle of returning to our vulnerable, tender beginnings. To me, embracing the side of us that is in touch with our emotions, never holding back our tears, is the greatest honor we can bestow upon ourselves.

Jordan Umphries

(actor, writer, sweater enthusiast)

There is a specific type of melancholy you feel in a vintage clothing store that only comes from having worked in one for some time. Though I am a lifelong thrifter and vintage shopper, it wasn't until I was a buyer and a manager for a vintage store that I realized how emotional the experience could be. Every single item that you appraise, style, and sell is something someone loved once. That dress was someone's favorite, that necklace was an anniversary gift, and someone got their heart broken in those shoes.

At a buy counter in any kind of resale shop, a fair portion of your business is the bereaved. Letting go of someone's things, whatever the reason, is a crucial part of the grieving process most of us don't ever think about. What do you do with the entire life someone has left behind? For many, money is a strong motivator. Funeral costs, hospital bills, and debt are all things we inherit alongside the tangibles like clothing, jewelry, and furniture. Financial need aside, though, what all of these sellers really want is the same thing: to know that things that were valuable to someone they loved are seen as valuable to someone else. Some sellers can't stomach the appraisal part of the process and return only when an offer is ready, but many actively participate in the process, giving every single item a backstory or special memory, haggling over pieces they believe hold higher value.

It is impossible not to be moved and occasionally overwhelmed by the history carried in each of their items. How do you take the history of a person and assign a numbered cost to it? From the niece desperately trying to sell her uncle's leather collection to cover his funeral costs, to the siblings who found their brother's collection of over one hundred vintage rock concert tees weeks after his death and hoped other collectors would love them; from the daughters who took ten years to let go of their mother's abundance of costume jewelry and Ferragamos, to the woman who tried three times to sell her mother's coats but couldn't do it: I remember all of you and your tears.

But more than any of them, I remember the widower who came in alone, who with a trembling lip softly touched and smelled every one of his wife's things one last time before letting them go, and who held my hand and thanked me for my time and my patience. It was the first and only time I let myself cry with someone at the buy counter, in full view of the rest of the store. After, I hugged him tightly, and he left. I hope that man found some peace after the experience. I hope they all did in their own ways.

Adam Voith

(music agent, writer, editor of Little Engines *magazine)*

I read the book about crying from 2019. I found it moving but didn't see myself inside.

I made my son cry last week. Made my wife cry recently. My therapist cried not long ago when I asked if she thought I was making progress. I'm certainly better at making people cry than crying for myself. I'm not proud of that, but at some point the balance sheet can't be denied.

Malory cries easily. It can be something beautiful, or podcasts, a memory; not always me.

When my mom came down to Bloomington to tell me the news—cancer—she cried and half wailed, "O! My sweet baby boy!"

I was dry as a bone, I'm afraid to say, thinking, *Who?*

It's been more than a decade, but I'm still waiting to cry. Since she passed, I've welled up or straight-up bawled countless times over other things. Mostly songs, sometimes commercials. There's that Big Thief performance on *Colbert*. That one gets me every time.

Kat Vollono

(psychotherapist)

Uncertainty and stress tends to accompany travel—tying up loose ends at work before a vacation, visiting family members, traffic on the way to the airport, worrying about a pricey hotel, and making sure the kids aren't about to blow a fuse. Feeling tears begin to flow is not unusual when we feel stressed and anxious. Crying is a meaningful release for us, activating our parasympathetic nervous system, which regulates and relaxes our body after periods of stress.

The plane's norms force us to be quiet and contemplative, disconnecting from the buzz of the external and reconnecting to our internal world. Reconnection invokes mindfulness, which, at times, may accompany crying. If we haven't had time in our busy daily lives to hold space for grief, transition, fear, or sadness, we are particularly vulnerable to the stillness of the airplane.

Symbolically, the plane mirrors an alchemical and womblike experience. You enter the plane's belly—at the mercy of the pilots, flight attendants, the weather, the snorer, the cat under the seat howling—until you reach your destination. After a period of incubation, you appear in a completely new environment, born into an opportunity to start anew, bigger and better than you were previously.

If the plane is an alchemical process, turning metal into gold, darkness into light, what else can come with transformation but tears?

Dana Wachs

(film and dance composer, audio engineer, cool aunt)

Crying at the speed of sound.

The first memory I have of crying resulted from physical pain—a sudden ringing from an ear infection pitched a deafening, high-frequency tone that dominated my entire skull. When I say "deafening," I literally became suddenly—though temporarily—deaf. I must have been five or six, and for the next two weeks, I lived without a sound. Which makes it strange that I became an audio engineer—mostly mixing live music—for a living.

That brief trauma seems to have conditioned a heightened emotional response to aural stimulation. I've cried after a balloon burst near me, but also I've cried watching the Dirty Three perform. I've cried in silence, as the enormity of sonic possibilities overwhelmed my sense of intention, and I've cried at concerts, grateful to be led through a composer's intimate path to resolution and absorbing sound pressure levels that left me physically exhausted.

The mind-body connection, the flexing of muscle and memory, coupled with the willful surrender to the emotional manipulation of art, all seem forever intertwined for me as a result of that brief illness. In a public display of crying, I do not feel embarrassed at the

emotional vulnerability my tears reveal (to myself, and to those in my vicinity). More so, I feel
grateful to be in cathartic compatibility with a
triggered synapse, to be moved by these intan-
gible but visceral environments of my choosing.
Tones, textures, tears.

Shy Watson

(writer, author of Horror Vacui*)*

#1

I was sixteen and I didn't want to play soccer so I offered to give him a blow job instead. I got on my knees, unzipped his pants, and coaxed it into my teenage mouth. I'd been at it for a few minutes before his mom walked in. She shielded her eyes, then told us to leave. I sobbed in the car. He drove me to a labyrinth because he had once been to a different labyrinth where he talked with God. God had told him great things, prophecies. Some of which involved money. I kicked my ankles onto the dashboard and sunk into the seat. My convulsions caused the seat belt to lock up, feet pressed against the windshield until it split. The crack looked like lightning. My breath sped from my lungs. When his mom asked what happened, he told her a rock fell from an overpass. But she wasn't an idiot. She knew it was me.

#2

His grave didn't yet have a headstone, though his mother showed me pictures of the one she ordered online. It was black marble, and his name was chiseled in as Jeff! Bess! He would have approved. Her husband drove us to the family cemetery.

We stood at the freshly dug, decorated dirt. She showed me where his head was in relation to his feet. I pressed my palms to the earth. I moved the whole way down like a massage. It felt calm below. His mother asked if  I wanted to hang out with him alone, but before I could answer, she walked away. First, I laid on my side with my arm stretched six feet above his chest. Then, I rolled facedown onto the dirt. I said what I thought he would want to hear, which was what I would want to hear. My mouth and eyes bubbled until the earth turned to mud. When I stood, I could feel it caked against my cheeks. I wanted a sleeping bag. It would have been nice.

Jamieson Webster

(psychoanalyst, professional mourner)

Freud uses the German word *schreien*—which means crying out, bawling, wailing, screeching, yelling, and which has been translated into English as "screaming" in the standard edition of his works—to denote a special class of representations in the mind that link a sound (screaming) to a perception in the outside world. He writes, "When otherwise, owing to pain, one has received no good indication of the quality of the object, the information of one's own scream serves to characterize the object. . . . the first class of conscious memories has been created. Not much is now needed in order to invent speech." Freud is trying to lay down a scientific system, a first explanation for the organization of neurons in the brain according to pain and pleasure, memory and conscious perception, word and object representations. What he posits in this early text, *Project for a Scientific Psychology* (1895), is speculative, radical, and fascinating: the idea that the origin of speech is crying, pain, and the failure of others to relieve this pain.

We are, in the Freudian universe, utterly helpless as humans, especially as human infants. All we can do is scream and cry, remember screaming and crying. Little by little, this becomes an act of judgment over the environment as hostile or unhelpful: the absence and betrayal of others, whether they can provide satisfaction and relief. These representations will develop into the wish to communicate, but also the *ability* to do so. Linking sound and image is the very basis of language and something that separates us from the rest of the animal kingdom. Through language, we are more able to get the help we need. While this end goal feels like a kind of redemption, we should remember that by the time we can communicate (it takes us quite a long time), we need less help than we once did.

This discrepancy is our impetus to help others, to respond to their cries. Their tears awaken in us the memory of our own and is the foundation for empathy. Freud writes, "In this way, this path of discharge acquires a secondary function of the highest importance, that of *communication*, and the initial helplessness of human beings is the *primal source of all moral motives*." In the Freudian mind, remembering, wishing, and judging form a triumvirate that he calls "useless" because they do nothing to change reality— they are a reaction to crying. Communication (namely, speech) and help (responding to the other's helplessness) do change reality— they are actions, which develop out of crying.

If you will allow me one last diversion, we can see this Freudian paradigm powerfully in Joan Didion's book *The Year of Magical Thinking*, where she spends the year following her husband's death going over all the details. She tries to figure out what could have been done differently, or who should have done what, or known what, along with all of her final memories of him. All of this, she comes to understand, was masking her utter helplessness in the face of loss, and was a final, magical attempt to keep him alive. As I read the final pages, where she realizes this, I felt myself giving way to a flood of tears. This process became the book, one that I know has immeasurably helped others who have lost loved ones.

Lillie West

(musician, artist, performs as Lala Lala)

Am I Supposed to Think About It or Avoid Thinking About It

Experiencing grief everywhere I go
At the dentist
Peeling an orange in the car
What's unfinished business?
The shape of your jaw, put away for years
6 stories down

Zoe Whittall

(novelist, TV writer; her latest books are
The Spectacular *and* The Fake*)*

The first time it happens I'm standing beside the first girl to kiss me in a way that broke through my ambivalence about having a body. We're in a crowd of mostly women, or to be more historically accurate, womyn. (It's the late nineties, an embarrassingly earnest time of my life.) The crowd starts chanting "No Justice, No Peace!" and I whisper it at first, feeling shy to hear my own voice join the chorus of others. It's the same feeling I had singing hymns in church as a kid, wanting my voice to blend but instead hearing its sharp, uncertain tones loudly in my own ears. The woman beside me shouts with gusto.

Something about the chanting chokes me up and tears come to my eyes involuntarily. It shocks me, to be crying with no sadness and no clear emotional trigger, and to start in the middle of the cry, no gradual buildup of tears or growing heat across my face to warn me of what's to come. I knuckle my closed eyes, look away from my date, willing the tears to stop. I couldn't explain them if asked. Then someone at the megaphone begins a searing speech and more tears come, accompanied by a gulp, a sob I try to soften. Am I going crazy? I'm not sad; perhaps I'm moved? But I don't really feel moved, intellectually. This crying is my body acting on its own, without reason or permission.

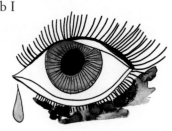

The next day we drive to see Sleater-Kinney perform in a gymnasium in Syracuse. We are underslept, drinking wine from a re-purposed soda bottle, and when the crowd goes wild in cheers and applause at the end of "I Wanna Be Your Joey Ramone" it happens again—sudden, sharp tears. The clapping in unison, the chorus of it all, triggers them. This time everyone is looking at Carrie Brownstein's swagger, and I can disguise this discordant reaction, mascara rivering down my face carried by what could plausibly be sweat. It confuses me because, at this time in my life, my emotional state volleys mostly between anxiety or a vague contentedness. I feel fear, or lack of fear. Perhaps there's occasionally drunk, or sad, or jealous watching the woman above with another girl, or embarrassed making her mixtapes with lyrics scrawled in pen on white cardboard, like "don't say another word about the other girl." But I am mostly fine. Often happy. But something about the feeling, the sound, the sensory experience of a crowd of people uniting in applause, cheers, or chanting prompts tears that should reasonably come at other moments, but often don't.

It happens like this for the rest of my life—at concerts, protests, weddings, karaoke, even—anytime a crowd acts as one. I wonder sometimes if it is evolutionary in some way, a relic of a former brain. Eventually, my mother tells me this happens to her as well. It's an inherited tick. Now I'm able to say to whoever is around me, "This happens in crowds, I'm not sure why," and some find it curious and others banal. At times, if I haven't cried in a while, I'll use it as an opportunity to release the pent-up emotions that have grown more varied since the age of nineteen, when being cool was a thing I thought a person could be.

Brock Wilbur

(journalist, editor in chief of the alternative news publication The Pitch *in Kansas City, Missouri)*

wrote for film and TV. I toured the country as a stand-up comedian. I was one of the first journalists to break the story of the NXIVM (alleged) sex cult. I helped script the biggest online video game in the world. I've lived a life that seems scattershot on the page, but all of these paths share two consistent themes. One: most creative fields are designed to encourage you to lean on an addiction—ope. Two: the most important skill set a person can develop is the process of telling a story. Not just regurgitating facts but enacting a reliable moment for those who never would have shared that space. In journalism, I find that the arc of the moral universe is long, but it bends toward pain.

I adore what I do, as a fierce (and occasionally quite loud) champion of the truth living in one of the best cities in the country. That doesn't mean that I have purely good days, ever. Eighty-five percent of the calls I make contain the phrase, either at the start or at the end, "It is incredible to meet you and holy shit I wish this had happened under different circumstances." I go to a therapist now who also treats ambulance drivers. She says that we use the same language and that behind the scenes we secretly react in the same way. We acknowledge to a person that they are nice, human, and worthy of love—or at least understanding. And, on some level, we nod to the fact that we are meeting them at the lowest moment of their lives.

Some nights, when I cry in my office while replaying a day's interviews, I feel jealousy for those ambulance drivers. They drop someone off at a hospital, and professionals immediately start saving them. In journalism, there are equal "worst days of your life" that cross your path, but you can never know—or promise—that some form of justice will follow. At least once a week, I ask a person to relive the worst moment of their entire life, and the best that I can offer is—when it breaks me enough—starting to audibly choke up, and then apologize for the world we live in.

I was told when I took this job that I should divorce myself from emotional reactions. In that way, I'm terrible at what I do. But I believe that if someone willingly shares their pain with you, the least you can do is receive it in kind.

Darcie Wilder

(writes and lives in Hell's Kitchen with her chihuahua mix, Coco)

At some point I began crying less from self-pity. I began crying for more ambiguous reasons like "being moved"; something dramatic and intense but not specifically upsetting. Maybe I
had exhausted the energy spent on emoting bereavement, maybe I
was tired or maturing. There was also crying as a physical response
to stimuli constructed by commercial industries: business models
based on finding the right combination of sound and visuals, words
and tone and timing to elicit goose bumps. Like a doctor knocking a
knee for the kick reflex, an advertisement for blood pressure medication or sneakers could stir the synapses connected to the smell of
a New England summer during the last days of camp and create an
uncontrolled, yet reliable, physical response.

Titanic was in theaters around the same time as *Paulie*, an un-
derappreciated movie about a bereft, wayward parrot. One of my
third-grade classmates (or maybe it was me) spoke of someone who
cried during *Paulie* but not *Titanic*. It was a big novelty, the idea
that movies were stand-ins for the facts of events: real century-old
mass death and fictionalized avian grief; that sadness could be mea-
sured via emoting; that any of it meant anything. Part of it was the

mystery of adults "crying from happiness" during older, boring, more "adult" events, like a wedding. Now it seems more like "crying from being moved."

Because at the end of *Paulie*, after finding his long-lost love, Marie, no longer a stuttering little girl, he sees his cut feathers regrown, and finds he can yet again soar above her garden and land back on her arm. Hope!

Maybe "crying from being moved" is about being upset in a positive way, a positive emotional disturbance. Someone once asked me to make a sadness-themed playlist and it led to an existential crisis, in which I tried to reconcile that feeling sad because you were feeling your feelings was "good" or "healthy," and so sadness was, in a way, happiness?

So now I cry less from sadness and more from "being moved," and I'm still unsure what that means. It was how adults cried. They were "so happy they cried," when I only knew about crying from skinned knees, disappointment, and embarrassment. From being hurt, I guess. As an adult it's less for "joy" or "happiness" and more from over-whelm—feeling small at the incredible complexity of the world and of human relationships, awe at the pliability of relationships, reconciliation after rupture, the miracle of repair. Maybe crying as a kid had been from the awe of the magnitude of the world around me—the terror of being small—and crying as an adult is from an awe of the magnitude of the universe, of being outweighed by adversity but still, somehow, proof of the possibility of re-silience—not my own strength, but a grace.

Alan Wyffels

(musician, member of Perfume Genius)

My grandma was my favorite person in the world. I did not cry at my grandma's funeral. I am now on a plane watching Julia Roberts as Erin Brockovich advocate for a promotion and the tears are streaming down my face. Is something misfiring up there? Is there a science behind why we turn into sniveling messes the moment we reach ten thousand feet? Someone recently asked me if I am a "crier," and I didn't know how to answer that. I certainly do not feel like a "normal" crier. I have had tearless spells that have lasted five years, yet I've also cried every day for weeks on end. I can listen to an entire record with explicit lyrics about grief and loss and not shed a single tear. However, some days I can sit at the piano, simply play the plagal cadence of IV to I (known as the "Amen" chords), and this will be enough to get me bawling. It seems as though the

RX # 1234567
FOR - EVERY ONE
ONCE A DAY FOR A
GOOD CRY
MAKES THE WORLD A
BETTER PLACE - REFILL∞

demented gatekeeper of my tears is playing a twisted game with me. I wish there was a pressure point we could squeeze, some sort of pill or potion we could take, to initiate crying on demand. A prescription of a daily cry would make the world a much better place, don't you think?

Tamara Yajia

(writer, comedian)

When I was five years old, my uncle Raul was going to take me to the Teatro Gran Rex, in Buenos Aires, to see a theater production of *My Little Pony*. He was due to pick me up in an hour, and my mom was helping me get dressed for the occasion. Earlier that morning I had watched an episode of *Alf* where the daughter, I think her name was Lynn, was wearing a red T-shirt with a pocket on it. I thought it was a really cool look. Simple. Red T-shirt. Pocket on the front. Timeless. So I sat on my bed and told my mom I wanted to wear a red T-shirt with a pocket on it to go to the theater. My mom looked through my closet and told me I didn't own a red T-shirt with a pocket on it. I did, however, own a red T-shirt with Alf's face on it. Perfect! She pulled it out and showed it to me. I didn't want that. I wanted a red T-shirt with a pocket on it. My mom said that wouldn't be possible. The closest I could get to my desired look was the red T-shirt with Alf's face on it. She told me to try it on. It would look great. I put it on and I hated it. It was not at all what I wanted. Not even close to the look I was going for. I started to throw a tantrum. I needed a red T-shirt with a pocket on it to be acquired for me and it was not being acquired. I felt rage. I felt hatred. I began weeping unconsolably at the unfairness of the situation. My mom was fucking done with me. She called my dad over. *There is no red shirt with a pocket on it, and that's that.* I was now pounding on my pillow, screaming, sobbing. It was unreal. It was unacceptable. My dad said, "That's it. You're done. You're not going to the theater. No *My Little Pony* for you." My parents called Uncle Raul and told him not to pick me up. My rage became so extreme that I grabbed a Care Bear stuffed animal and attempted to rip its arm off with my teeth. My parents grabbed me and put me in a cold shower until I calmed down. Sitting on the shower floor, soaking wet, and choking out words through the tears, I attempted to explain to them, for one last time, that I just wanted a red T-shirt with a pocket on it. The next day my parents put me into therapy.

Tasha Young

(writer, author, music lover)

I t is dangerous to cry while driving. For the longest time, I believed it was dangerous to cry at all. I don't cry very often, I think in part because I learned at an early age that showing emotions could get me into trouble, and because I had been put on antidepressants as a teenager, in response to very reasonable causes of misery. In my twenties, I tried to go off them once or twice. During those short-lived trials, I'd start crying a lot, as if making up for all the years I could not cry. This crying was so unfamiliar and alarming I'd go back to the doctor, whose face it seemed couldn't decide between compassion and "I told you so."

At thirty-two, after a few years of successful therapy, I began to feel that I could trust myself, that I could feel my feelings and my life wouldn't crumble. The summer that I completed a long, gradual tapering and weaned off of the pills entirely, I rented a car and went on a road trip from Brooklyn to Maine, where I was born and raised. Swimming in the sea, eating lobster and oysters, reconnecting with relatives; I gently put my emotional spectrum to the test. But I was overcome most often while driving alone.

I ventured into the realm of emotional living with a tool kit of techniques like a little scientist of the lived experience. With some trepidation, I clung to the coping skills my therapist had taught me: mindfulness, self-compassion, somatic experiencing. As a writer, I was most interested in the practice of describing the physical sensation of my emotions, without spinning a story around them. The goal was simply to relate to my feelings without panicking that something was wrong with me for feeling so much.

I was dazzled by the lucid experience of how crying feels in the body. Like a flood in my chest, and a tightness that seemed to emanate from my spine right behind my sternum and grip me from the inside. I imagined my chest as a hollow cavity filled with the warm salt water that was now brimming at the orifices in my head. The emotional cues were physically jarring, both unfamiliar and like coming home to myself. It was, to my surprise, a spiritual experience—another theretofore foreign concept.

Driving while listening to music was the surest way to trigger tears. The pressure from inside my chest built until I could barely speak, let alone sing. But I felt the need to sing along to the music I was listening to, to release the pressure. As I drove through the forests of coastal Maine, my voice opened some flue and the tears flowed. My chest heaved it out, and once my voice broke, I knew I had to pull over. This happened several times during my road trip that summer, and I was grateful. It felt amazing.

I still don't cry very often, but not because I am ashamed or afraid, not anymore. I understand now that to feel is a gift, and to cry is a pleasure.

Acknowledgments

Writing a book can feel pretty solitary, but it takes a community, and *Sad Happens* never would have moved from a tweet to a full-fledged book without the help of a number of people. My most immediate, beloved, and important community is my family: Thanks to my wife, Jane, and our sons, Henry and Jake, for being there, always. (Credit, too, to our dog, Pete, and pet frogs, Tad and Veiny.) Endless appreciation, also, to my father, who, like my mother, always told me it was okay to show emotion. Thanks to my agent, Chad Luibl, for agreeing that the original idea had legs. Major thanks to my old pal Rose Lazar for jumping in so enthusiastically to illustrate, expand upon, and better that idea—and for not killing me when this thing moved from 40 contributors to 115. (She and I have wanted to work together on a project since we lived in Buffalo twenty-plus years ago—I'm so glad to finally see it happen as *Sad Happens*.) Of course, many thanks to all the contributors for so graciously sharing their stories. And thank you to the wonderful team at Simon & Schuster: editing wizards Stephanie Frerich and Emily Simonson along with production editor Morgan Hart, interior designer Ruth Lee-Mui, production manager Allison Har-zvi, marketer Tyanni Niles, and publicist Shannon Hennessey. (See, what I said about community is true: We're nearing 150 people for one book.) And, thanks to you, it goes without saying, for reading this far.

—BRANDON STOSUY

In a time and place in history where emotions have been running high and tight for a few years, I'd like to thank everyone who shared a tale of tears with us to make this book happen. Reading and getting to illustrate an emotional time stamp on your lives was a privilege and a joy. Thank you to Brandon Stosuy. We met many years ago, and I think we already knew at some point we'd work together on a project, and the fact that the one we worked on ended up being about crying makes all the sense in the world. Thanks to Chad Luibl, our agent on this project, for your belief in it and for helping us see it through and transforming it into something we didn't expect it to turn into. We're better for it. Thanks to the team at Simon & Schuster—Emily and Stephanie—who were so supportive and encouraging of this emotional breakthrough. From my life and beyond I want to thank all the people, places, and things that inform what have made me cry. I cry a lot, I cry easily, and the universe at large and all of my life's experiences have made me that way for good or for worse, but always for the better. Thanks to Rob, a.k.a. Robert Aiki Aubrey Lowe, for always inspiring and supporting me to do whatever I want. It's a rare quality in a partner that I don't take for granted. Thanks, Violet.

—ROSE LAZAR

About the Authors

BRANDON STOSUY is the cofounder and editor in chief of *The Creative Independent*, published by Kickstarter. He previously worked as director of editorial operations at *Pitchfork*. Brandon curates the annual Basilica Soundscape festival in Hudson, New York, and has been a music curator at both MoMA PS1 in New York City and the Broad museum in Los Angeles. He is the author of three books on creativity, *Make Time for Creativity*, *Stay Inspired*, and *How to Fail Successfully*, and two children's books, *Music Is . . .* and *We Are Music*. He lives in Brooklyn with his wife and two children.

ROSE LAZAR has a background in fine art and printmaking, and has published a number of art books. She founded Cosmic Peace Studio (formerly The Great Lakes Goods) in 2008, which is a paper and home goods line made in her studio in Brooklyn. Cosmic Peace Studio started as a way for Rose to continue her love of printmaking and has turned into a world of posi vibes and lucky totems for you and your home. In 2017 she started Adventures LTD Press with Robert Aiki Aubrey Lowe as a limited-edition art and music imprint and has published twenty (plus) editions and exhibited in art book fairs throughout the United States.